Doll Fashion Anthology and Price Guide

Featuring:
Barbie®
Tammy™
Tressy®,

et al

by

A. Glenn Mandeville

Hobby House Press™

Published by   Cumberland, Maryland 21502

Dedication

This book is dedicated to the most talented person I have ever met, Dick Tahsin. His love of art, his love of life and his love for *Barbie*® inspired this book. Enthusiasm is a great motivator! Thank you Dick, from the bottom of my heart!

Acknowledgements

Some very special people helped on this project. Sarah Eames, the "Queen of Barbie;" Bob Gantz, photographic assistance; Donna Felger, my Editor; Candace Irving, Public Relations at Mattel, Inc.; Franklin Lim Liao, Dick Tahsin and Robert Tonner.

Additional copies available at $9.95 each plus $1.25 postage from
Hobby House Press, Inc.
900 Frederick Street
Cumberland, MD 21502
or from your favorite bookstore or dealer.

ISBN: 0-87588-318-4

Table of Contents

Introduction

The registered trademarks, the trademarks and the copyrights appearing in italics within this introduction belong to Mattel, Inc., unless otherwise noted.

If you are currently in your late 30s, you are a lucky person indeed! Over the past 28 years, starting in 1959, the world of pop culture, fashion and traditional sex roles of men and women have all gone through a radical transformation. The "baby boomers," (classified by psychologists as those now 21 to 40s),are the largest and the most spoiled group in history. Born of mothers from the Great Depression and fathers from World War II, they were the first generation in this country to grow up in a world relatively free from war and poverty. Much hope, time, money and expensive educations were put into this group of babies. Their parents hoped they would never want for anything.

All this spare time led to these children developing, in the late 1950s, their own culture, namely that of the "teenager." Up until this time children were little more than young adults, waiting to grow up into the boring world of work and obligations. The baby boomer children wanted and got more! A wonderful period in their lives developed as they reached 13, and soon an entire nation was living a life of daily "fads," created for the boom children. The world of a teenager was certainly an awesome place.

Children that today we call "pre-teens," approached this time with both joy and anxiety. Those with "bubbly" personalities, "budding" figures, pretty faces and a wealthy family certainly had little to fear. The prepubescent whose life was not so enriched had some dread. BOTH, however, needed

Revlon Dolls® is a registered trademark of Hasbro, Inc.

"lessons," as it were, to prepare for "teenhood." For some unfortunates, the world of pizza parties, soda shops and hotrods would never come. For others, these rituals needed much preparation. Suddenly little girls, especially, wanted to begin preparing for this magical time early, to better their chances of success as a teenager. (Boys were more fortunate because athletic ability was still in the passport to teen acceptance at this time, but would change later on).

This need to prepare for the future spawned an entire new generation of dolls, — the fashion doll! "Big sister" dolls with "full" figures, (consisting of huge breasts and hourglass waists) took over the place of baby and toddler dolls. The Ideal Toy Corp. was a leader in the field with the *Revlon Dolls*, which taught a young girl her first lessons in high heels and makeup. This all led, in 1959, to the epitome of the fashion doll, *Barbie*.

When first released, *Barbie* seemed the answer to many a young girl who longed to have the life-style *Barbie* seemed to thrive on. Through playing with *Barbie*, a young girl could discover the world of modeling, adventure and those mysteries such as lingerie, jewelry, hairstyles and makeup. The personal life of *Barbie...Teen-age Fashion Model* seemed threatening to only a handful of parents, as most mothers seemed eager to live through their daughters the proms, dates and dresses that the depression and war took away. *Barbie* seemed to be the answer to every prayer a pre-teen girl might have.

5

As the years rolled by, social changes came rapidly. Influences in fashion and morals came from such unlikely sources as the White House, a la Jacqueline Kennedy, and Carnaby Street in London, via Twiggy — the Mod Model. Teenagers were evolving and Barbie was changing with them. As children grew up and eased into "teendom," Barbie and her boyfriend, Ken, and other friends were right there with up-to-the-minute advice on life-styles and fashions. Mattel spent millions to develop and perfect the personality traits that Barbie possessed. By the late 1960s, the "Gidget" type of personality, that of a pretty, talented, sensitive, but down-to-earth girl, was the American dream.

When the "British Invasion" occurred after the arrival of the Beatles, Barbie again was a trend setter. As the Women's Movement took women into athletics and career moves, Barbie again helped ease the tensions of social change in her young owners.

Many young adults today, myself included, can nostalgically view a panorama of our lives through a collection of Barbie dolls and her fashions. If you were actually doing all the things Barbie was, then your view is parallel to hers, in that you can say, "I had an outfit just like that!" If fate kept you from these trends, then you can join them, still in progress within the fantasy of your own collection.

To many collectors, Barbie represents a reality and a reminder of the lives they lived. To others, it is a fantasy world they would like to have known. Whatever the reason, Barbie is like an old high school yearbook, better because she is three dimensional!

Naturally, any person or object at the top that is successful is widely imitated, in order to capitalize on the money and fame that such a position includes. Other toy companies saw a great opportunity to cash in on the teen fashion doll trend.

Some were frankly awful, merely shadows of Barbie. Others, like Ideal's Tammy, American Character's Tressy, and Remco's Judy Littlechap, took a direction all their own, and now, with our educated backward glances, we see them for the brilliant social statement they make. Often neglected by Barbie collectors, these dolls show yet another view of life in the early 1960s, a time that can never again be equaled.

Come share with me now a view of our lives, glancing backward almost three decades! Through the teenage fashion doll, our fantasies and realities mix together in a most pleasant journey. Hopefully, this book will make you smile, laugh, reminisce, and perhaps shed a tear. Most of all, it will make you remember, or meet for the very first time, a wonderful era in which to be young and alive.

Tammy® is a registered trademark of the Ideal Toy Corp.
Tressy® is a registered trademark of American Character Doll Co.
Judy Littlechap® is a registered trademark of Remco.

How to Collect Teen Fashion Dolls

As many people collect teen fashion dolls as there are dolls themselves! Collector groups and fan clubs exist all over the world. Fashion and design interest many different people from all walks of life, from those who are personally involved in the fashion world, to the most casual observer. One thing they all share, however, is their love for these little pieces of perfection.

Recently, at a *Barbie* doll convention, a gathering held once a year for dedicated fans of this American icon, I could not help but notice the diverse group of collectors: high fashion models mixed with construction workers; handicapped chatted with athletes, "macho" men laughed with ballerinas; they all shared one common interest, *Barbie*!

Barbie's fans range in age from the three-year-old receiving her first doll to a senior citizen who never heard of "The Twist." Her appeal reaches all parts of the world, where she is viewed in the ethnic guise of that particular country.

To many collectors, the fashions are the real reason they collect. Issued by the hundreds over the years, they are the gravy, the sauce, as it were, that makes the dish come alive. Mannequin-like in form, *Barbie* is to many, NOT the personality that some envision, but merely a dressmaker's figure upon which talented individuals have draped dreams over the years. To this group, the little gloves, hats and purses are like religious tokens, treasured and saved, carefully matched to each outfit.

Another group of perfectionists want, and are willing to pay for, the unopened package which contains the story of *Barbie* as much as the object sealed inside. Never has a company put so much into a box as did Mattel. The fabulous artwork and the creative packaging all add to the story of a beautiful girl's wonderful life. Yet these items bring a premium price on the collectors' circuit, because *Barbie* was meant to be played with and few early dolls and fashions survive in this condition. Those that do disappear rapidly into the ever growing numbers of private collections of those who only want mint-in-box items, driving the prices ever skyward in a spiral of supply and demand.

There are those collectors who want the glamorous gowns and sensational sheaths displayed on *Barbie* dolls where they can be viewed in three-dimensional form. Under a dome, or in a cabinet, an early *Barbie* doll, lavishly dressed, is like "stealing" a memory right out of the past and trapping it under glass for all eternity. This type of collector wants to see the garment in motion.

Thus, as there are hundreds of different *Barbie* dolls, there are just as many ways to collect. Add to this the *Barbie* family over the years, beginning with boyfriend *Ken*, and girlfriend *Midge*, and continuing with the current best friend *Whitney*, and you can see how space and money have made collectors specialize either in a particular period that they fondly remember, or a certain doll, such as just *Barbie*. Some men, angry at being denied *Ken* dolls by a sexist society, now vigorously collect *Barbie's* male counterpart and his adventuresome outfits.

Like alphabet soup, the fashion doll world is made up of many diverse people and collections. The collector soon must decide on a way to go with his/her collection!

Thus exists a unique situation to collectibles, a market within a market, generated mainly by different tastes and the overwhelming number of items available. If one were to collect "everything," and that includes licensed products from toothbrushes to bobby pins, one would literally have to turn over the entire house to one's dolls! Indeed, many collectors have done just that, bewildering friends and relatives who cannot understand why. The collector, on the other hand, smiles secretly and hopes the viewer of the collection has something in HIS/HER life that brings as much happiness.

The collector of *Barbie* and other dolls, fashions and accessories ideally should have a random sampling of boxed items because the artwork really does tell a tale of Americana as well as the dolls themselves. Then fill in the gaps with perfect outfits, with the correct accessories, displayed on the right year dolls, and the fashion story of three decades becomes complete. It is difficult at first to realize that the main piece of an outfit such as a ball gown is not where the value lies, but in the accessories. If only old vacuum cleaner bags had been saved, how many precious little necklaces and gloves would be rescued! It is these tiny cameras and travel folders, hankies and telephones, that added so much to an outfit and are so difficult to find today. The sum total of an original and complete outfit is worth so much more than the parts.

All of this only adds to the fun. Many collectors carry notebooks listing the parts and accessories they need to complete the little outfits that lovingly tell so much of our culture.

Decide on the message you want your collection to say; then figure out the best way to make it say just that! The world of the fashion dolls is an exciting place. Filled with nostalgia, romance, glamour and adventure, your collection can bring you much happiness. There are dolls and outfits available in every price range. The sheer numbers of objects manufactured make it a challange to put together an interesting collection.

If you have never thought of *Barbie*, *Tammy*, *Tressy*, et al, then read on! If you already collect, then perhaps this book will make you examine your hobby in a new light. It has been my experience that doll collectors seem just a little smarter and a little nicer than the average person. *Barbie*, of all the fashion dolls, belongs to the past and, because she is still going strong, the future is hers as well.

Some of the other dolls in our story are trapped in a time warp, destined to repeat over and over the images of the past.

Others, like Hasbro's *Jem*, and Creata's *Lace*, bring the fashion doll collector face to face with the looks of the future.

Whatever direction your collection takes, make it an outstanding display. Just like the French fashion dolls of so long ago, ages after we are all gone, a beautifully preserved doll, correctly dressed and coiffed, will tell future generations of our realities, our fantasies, our hopes and our dreams. As a fashion doll collector, we contribute much to the future. You ARE your collection. Make your dreams come true with an exciting collection of teen fashion dolls and their wardrobes!

The Care And Repair Of Teen Fashion Dolls

Some teen fashion doll collectors insist that all their dolls, clothing and accessories be never removed from box. Others enjoy the three-dimensional viewing of a mint doll dressed in a mint outfit. Still others buy played-with dolls and restore them, buying pieces of outfits, always looking for the right accessories. Many collectors, myself included, do all three! Some outfits simply look better displayed in the packaging. These outfits are usually ones that have a lot of small accessories such as trays, watermelon slices and spoons that are awkward to keep near your doll. Pieces can get lost, and so many prefer this type of outfit in the packaging.

The wonderful outfits from the couture period of the mid 1960s look fabulous on a doll, creating a three-dimensional trip backward in time! Sometimes the story on the packaging, along with the artwork is as interesting as the items inside!

The best collections, in my opinion, are made up of examples of items both in and out of the packaging. Some boxes tell the story of American fashion perfectly, and some outfits do the same. As you will discover, an outfit or doll still sealed in the package is worth twice as much as one out! For this reason, it is foolish to open a perfect old outfit. Not only that, but the collector of the future deserves to have some perfect examples left from our discoveries.

Teen fashion dolls are sturdy little dolls that basically were fashion mannequins. For that reason, many have survived with just superficial problems. You, as a collector, have to be able to see beneath the dirt and discover the treasure that is hidden! It is very rewarding to restore a *Barbie* or *Tammy* or *Tressy*, (or any doll for that matter), back to its original form.

The suggestions that follow may seem strange to you! Many may surprise you, and quite frankly, they are so easy to follow that I hate to tell "all," as it were, because we collectors are often able to buy many dolls inexpensively because the seller has not the talent nor the imagination to clean up the doll! All of these ideas are based on a lifetime of doll repair experience. The brand name products mentioned are not endorsements of that particular product or company, but simply are the ones available in my area that I have used with great success.

Tip number one is NEVER rush right home with a new purchase and start scrubbing! Live with the doll for a few days and get to know the faults and strengths before you begin any restoration project. Secondly, it is better to under restore than over restore an old doll. Some stains such as ballpoint pen ink, markers and grease just will not come out of vinyl. If you "treat" these stains too much, the color comes right out of the doll and you wind up with a worse situation. Do not buy a doll with these types of stains unless they are in an inconspicuous place.

These methods are for vinyl fashion dolls from all years and work very well. First, gather up several clean white towels, a roll of paper towels, cotton swabs, alcohol, a clean dry toothbrush, cleanser such as "Comet," a softer cleanser such as "Soft Scrub," a spray-on cleaner like "409," and liquid soap in a pump dispenser that is white like "Ivory." Additional supplies include shampoo, conditioner, plastic wrap, small orthodontic rubber bands, a metal hair pick that has a comb on the opposite end (available in dime stores), and perm wave rollers in the three smallest sizes.

IT IS MUCH EASIER TO HAVE ALL THESE ITEMS HANDY BEFORE YOU BEGIN. You can get dangerously distracted running all over the house later on, so have everything together. It is best to work on several dolls at a time, saving clothing for all at once also! You may need acrylic paints that say they can be used on vinyl such as "Flo-paque" and a small, fine quality brush for makeup touch-ups.

Let us say you have a ponytail doll that is filthy, but makeup seems intact. The legs have ground-in soil, there is a little green in her earring holes, and her hair is down and matted. BELIEVE IT OR NOT, SHE CAN BE RE- STORED TO ALMOST MINT!

Begin by washing the entire doll in the sink with liquid soap. Use a cotton swab to cleanse around facial features. Be gentle on facial makeup. Then start out with the soft cleanser and a paper towel, and try to remove the ground- in dirt on legs, arms and torso. Tougher dirt may require the regular cleanser. It will all come off! When the doll is clean, wash it again with the liquid soap and rinse well.

Dip a cotton swab in alcohol. Gently remove the head by tilting it to one side. Clean out the earring holes with the swab on both sides of the head. Replace the head.

Next, wash the ponytail in sham- poo; then pour a pea-sized blob of conditioner right into the hair. Use your metal hair pick to ease knots out of the hair. When it combs smoothly with the pick, switch to the comb end and work carefully again until all the hair is smooth. You should have one long strand that stands out from the rest of the hair at the bottom. This is for the wrap around the ponytail.

Turn the doll upside down and comb all the hair up into a ponytail that sits at the crown of the head. Secure with an orthodontic rubber band (no bigger than 1/4in [.65cm] diameter). Wrap the long strand around the ponytail, and on the underside of the ponytail, lift up the rubber band with the pick and push the hair strand under it. The ponytail will now be wrapped just as it was originally. Comb the rest of the hair down straight and roll up the ends in a perm wave roller. To "set" the hair, fill a juice glass with boiling water (using caution so as not to burn yourself) and prop the doll so just the roller sits in the water! The heat will put in the set. (This can be used on an entire head, such as restoring "flips" on *Midge*®, or other dolls.) Allow the water to cool to room temperature and remove the head from the water. Let it dry overnight, remove the roller, and your ponytail is just like when the doll left the factory!

You can use the drying time to check on other things. Sometimes facial soil is heavy. Use "409" on a paper towel to remove crusts around noses and in ears. A dry toothbrush can work out this dirt for you. If your doll is missing some makeup, touch it up with the above mentioned paints, using little strokes. Just keep saying to yourself that if a factory worker could do all this, so can I! Believe me, you can.

If you want to keep the earrings in the doll, you must dip them several times in Superglue. If you do not, the earring will turn the ear area green and the doll will be ruined.

These methods work on dolls from all periods. Just be sure to be gentle on facial areas, and keep the face out of the boiling water when setting hair using this method. (Plastic wrap can act as a hair net while the doll's head is in the boiling water.)

IT IS ALWAYS BETTER TO

PRACTICE THESE METHODS ON BASKET CASE DOLLS FIRST! Buy some real pieces of junk at a flea market and see what can be done. By doing this, you can get a feel for what can be restored, and what cannot. Remember that *Barbie* and other teen fashion dolls are really display mannequins for an outfit and that some imperfections are livable to most collectors.

Mattel clothing and some garments made by other manufacturers were the finest made for any doll during the 1960s! Even more expensive clothing, made in America, could not compare to the workmanship that went into these tiny garments. Most were made of natural fibers or satins, and can be restored quite easily. AGAIN, PRACTICE ON SOME OLD CLOTHING FIRST!

Gather together several flat pans like those used for lasagna. You will also need a non-chlorine bleach such as "Clorox 2," and a regular bleach. For dry cleaning, a tightly closed jar of cleaning fluid is necessary and a sewing kit helps for repairs.

Begin by examining the garment. If repairs are needed, this is the time to reinforce seams that have pulled and repair torn hemlines. Then determine if your garment is cotton or satin (taffeta as well). For satin gowns like *Barbie's Enchanted Evening*, dry cleaning is the only safe way to restore the dress. Fill a one quart glass jar with several bottles of cleaning fluid (available at most dry cleaners) and drop in the garment. Shake the jar and that will agitate the garment. When the garment looks clean, remove it quickly. Never leave the dress in more than a couple of minutes. As you remove the garment, it will dry before your eyes as the fluid evaporates. Use this time to hand shape the garment, stuffing the body part with crumbled paper towels to hold the shape. You can even use an old doll body if you like to help shape the garment. Do not use a good doll, as the fluid may discolor the doll when wet. If light ironing is needed, use a cool iron and press on the wrong side. REMEMBER, MORE DAMAGE IS DONE BY INCORRECT IRONING THAN BY WASHING.

If your garment is cotton, or synthetic, place first in some lukewarm water to wet the outfit. Then put a cup of non-chlorine bleach into the lasagna pan. Add enough water to fill and drop in the garment. Let the dress soak for about 30 minutes. White collars can be bleached with a watered down solution of 1/2 cup bleach to 2 cups water. Use cotton swabs to get just the solution on the right places.

Finally, rinse the garment in another pan. Shake out the excess water, and again hand shape, stuffing the dress to fit the doll. Place on a clean, white towel and let dry in the sun. Check every 15 minutes or so on the drying process so you can shape the outfit as it is drying. Done correctly, you can avoid most ironing which, as mentioned, gives a shiny, overdone look to the clothes.

Dirty shoes can be scrubbed with cleanser and a toothbrush. Plastic purses and accessories can be cleaned with "409." Remember, a little time spent now will result in an object you can display with pride for years to come!

Restoring teen fashion dolls can be a rewarding way to add new dolls to your collection without spending the money for a mint doll. Teen fashion doll collecting is so much fun because, unlike other areas of doll collecting, there are so many ways to collect the same thing! Proceed carefully and confidently and you will not go wrong! Why not add a "new" old doll to your collection today!

I. Barbie® And The History Of American Fashion

The registered trademarks, the trademarks and the copyrights appearing in italics within this chapter belong to Mattel, Inc., unless otherwise noted.

Pop culture began in the late 1950s. Movies featuring teenagers and their life-styles propelled them into a longing not for adulthood, but of a time of never-never land called "teendom." Thus, in 1959, *Barbie...The Teen-age Fashion Model* was born, with an entensive wardrobe of fashions mirroring the current trends of style. Through the years *Barbie* would continue to reflect fashion images and values of society. Fifties' evening gowns, swinging Sixties' minis, Seventies' bell-bottoms and halter tops, to the designer dresses of the Eighties, *Barbie* has shown it all in great style!

Barbie's wardrobe was designed at Mattel by Charlotte Johnson, (later known as C.J.). Inspired by haute couture, designers such as Balenciaga, Dior, Givenchy and Balmain served as the influnce behind *Barbie's* extensive styles from her inception through 1966. Her miniature garments of fine fabric came complete with tiny zippers, buttons, luxurious linings, sparkling jewelry and above all, a name to set the mood for the outfit. Titles such as *Easter Parade, Solo in the Spotlight* and *Gay Parisienne* exemplify this technique used by the French couture designers.

The quality of *Barbie's* outfits was mesmerizing, as was the attention to detail. Since her early garments were not mass-produced, the time and care could be given to detailing a piece to

1. The epitome of early 1960s evening wear. A *Ponytail Barbie* models *Enchanted Evening* (1960)', an ensemble inspired by Castillo.

2. This January 1950 *Vogue* cover clearly reflects "The Face" of the 1950s and early 1960s. Beauty was a subject of great importance and makeup helped enhance this. *Barbie's* early face mirrors this look of arched brows, side-glancing eyes and red hot lips!

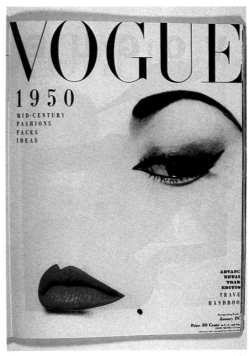

VOGUE

1950

MID-CENTURY
FASHIONS
FACES
IDEAS

ADVANC
RETAI
TRAD
EDITIO
TRAVE
HANDBOO

Price 30 Cents

utter perfection! The luxurious real silk full linings and hand-finished seams, hems and neatly sewn buttons gave *Barbie's* ensembles the look and quality of real haute couture. Logo signature labels were expertly sewn into each and every one!

Fashion in the 1950s was sophisticated and elegant. Women had to appear as though they had spent time making themselves perfectly groomed. ''Beauty'' became a subject of much importance now that wartime cosmetic shortages were over. Eyebrows were arched and darkened and lipstick gave the lips a hard line. Eye makeup varied from sultry brown to jade green; mascara was essential. Classic, yet simple hairstyles were the rule, swept up chignons worn with hats for daytime and evening, shoulder-length bobs for informal occasions. *Barbie* clearly reflected this look with her knowing arched brows, sultry side-glancing eyes, fire engine red lips and pert ponytail.

Before the mid 1960s, couture fashion took a dive into the sewing box and came up with quite a few ''threads,'' especially for *Barbie!* The polka-dotted silk taffeta, *Gay Parisienne* (1959) was a direct offspring of Hubert

---

3. The bubble dress was a mid-late 1950s fashion sensation. *Barbie* showed this trend in her 1959 polka-dotted *Gay Parisienne.*

4. Today the bubble dress is once again the fashion rage, as this publication reports.

5. *Barbie's* early fashions were inspired by haute couture designers. This 1965 *Barbie* ensemble *On the Avenue* shows the Dior influence of the tailored suit accompanied by the large collared jacket.

de Givenchy's 1956 sensation, the bubble dress. Today the bubble dress is once again the fashion rage. From Paris to the U.S., it can be seen in almost every designer's collection.

Tailored suits accompanied by jackets with large collars were very exemplary of the House of Dior's designer, Mark Bohan. *Barbie* ensembles such as *Fashion Luncheon* (1966), *Saturday Matinee* (1965) and *On The Avenue* (1965) show the Dior influence.

The great Balenciaga is clearly reflected in the outfit *Midnight Blue* (1964). Its fur collared, blue satin sleeveless cape, long white gloves and silver lamé clutch were typical accessories of Balenciaga. The 1963s *Career Girl* was yet another Balenciaga inspired ensemble. A smart, streetwise, houndstooth tweed suit, it was topped off by a matching cloche hat with rose, long black gloves and patent leather purse. This was a perfect outfit for *Barbie* to pursue her career as a fashion model.

The most popular millinery creation of all time, Balenciaga's "pillbox," was made famous by Jacqueline Kennedy, a combination of high-fashion model, movie star and royal queen. Prior to the 1960s, fashion influence had been exerted by movie stars and costume designers. *Imitation of Life* starring Lana Turner (1959), and *Back Street* starring Susan Hayward (1961) show a glittering array of "*Barbie*-like" fashions designed by Jean Louis. By the 1960s, the Hollywood star system was fading, as there were few actresses American women could emulate. Jackie Kennedy was the new clothes-conscious heroine. She spent $50,000 on her wardrobe the first 16 months after the election! Following her lead, women bared their arms to the shoulder and wore brightly colored, classic fashions. Because of Jackie,

women began wearing pillbox hats and this included *Barbie*! *Reception Line* (1965), *Theatre Date* (1963) and *White Magic* (1964) were just a few *Barbie* outfits that incorporated this millinery creation.

Barbie's most popular outerwear ensemble, *Red Flair* (1962), also came with a red velvet pillbox and flat bow. This Balenciaga-inspired coat came complete with an enormous sweep and melon sleeves.

Jackie Kennedy not only made the pillbox fashionable, but also a new bouffant coiffure known as the "bubble cut." Once again *Barbie* reflected this style, when in 1961 she was issued with not only a ponytail, but with this new style, as well!

Lurex, the metallic gold thread that swept through many fashions of the late 1950s and early 1960s, was seen on *Barbie* wearing *Evening Splendour* (1959), *Golden Elegance* (1963) and *Golden Glory* (1965).

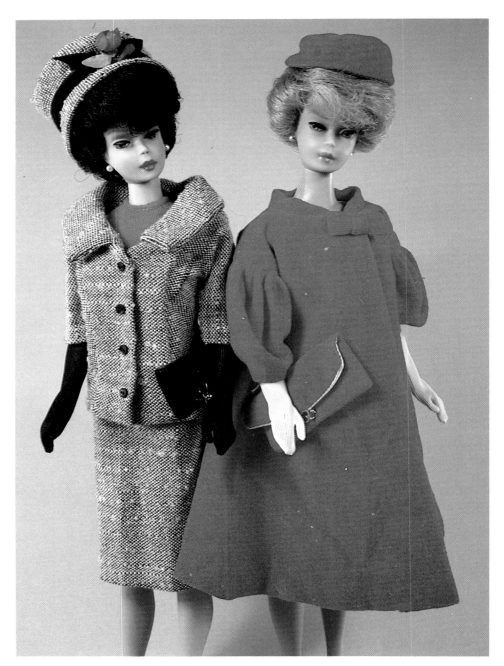

6. *Barbie* pays homage again to the great Balenciaga wearing the chic, tweed suit *Career Girl* (1963) (topped off by a cloche hat with rose) and the ravishing velvet *Red Flair* (1962) complete with the famous "pillbox."

Women's evening wear reflected the elegance and sophistication of this period, and so did *Barbie's*! Styles which ran the gamut from the black sheath and tulle flounce of *Solo In The Spotlight* (1960), (a homage to Charles James' "tulip" gown), to the pink flowing train of *Enchanted Evening* (1960), reminiscent of Castillo.

The popularity of ball gowns was never more apparent, be they ruffled, caped or bowed. *Barbie* showed this in such ensembles as the glamorous *Debutante Ball* (1966); the red ribbon bowed *Benefit Performance* (1966); the glittering *Magnificence* (1965); and the rabbit-stoled classic, *Junior Prom* (1965).

In the mid 1960s, fashion began to focus upon teenagers. For the first time, the fashion lead came from the young, not those in the mainstream. Fashion stopped being clothing and became a value, a tool, a way of life, a kind of symbolism. Styles changed so fast that manufacturers found it difficult to produce stock fast enough. Compared with the calmer Seventies, the Sixties seemed one frenetic dash to buy the latest "look." The "look" was that of young, free, swinging, energetic — "Mod!" (a euphemism for modern). *Barbie* symbolized this new look, when in 1967 she appeared on the scene with a whole new zesty personality and wearing the garment of the decade: the miniskirt.

Mary Quant's creation of the miniskirt in 1965 was a direct result of the youth rebellion. Skirt length was a provocative statement for women, as hair length was for men. If a woman bared her knee (or more), then she was instantly identified as being "Mod." If she chose to cover it, she was assumed to be square, dull and conservative.

"The more shocking the better!"

was the fashion statement of the late 1960s. Andre' Courregés was at the helm with such creations as the square-cut dress and flat white boots (later known as "go-go" boots). His influence was obvious in such *Barbie* outfits as *Zokko!* (1966) with its Courregés-style boots, and *Snap-Dash* (1966), a green mini trimmed in vinyl with a stylized western hat.

Paco Rabanne had shock appeal, too, with his chain-mail and plastic disc clothes, worn with huge plastic earrings. These earrings became high street fashion and *Barbie* donned them in her 1966 outfit, *Sunflower*.

The "see through look" of the late 1960s (revealing the body underneath) was interpreted in *Barbie's Jump Into Lace* (1966), a sleeveless white lace jumpsuit reminiscent of Andre' Courregés.

The popularity of the ultra-psychedelic mini over matching tights is clearly shown in *Barbie's* outfits *Drizzle-Dash* (1967), *Togetherness* (1968), *Mini-Prints* (1968) and *Tunic 'N Tights* (1968).

Mod prints, proclaiming "Flower Power," could be seen in *Barbie* wearing *Bouncy Flouncy* (1967), *Swirly-Cue* (1968) and *Flower Wower* (1970). *Festival Fashion* was a Woodstock inspired ensemble, complete with balloon pants, fringed belt, ruffled blouse, vest and bandana head scarf. *Barbie* only needed her long hair strewn with flowers to give this hippy outfit the perfect touch!

By the end of the 1960s, the original mini had been replaced by the "micro," which climbed up the leg until it was almost thigh-high!

The fashion establishment, who was never too keen on the mini idea, fought back. Instead of the mini or the ankle-length maxi, they proposed a compromise: the midi (middle of the

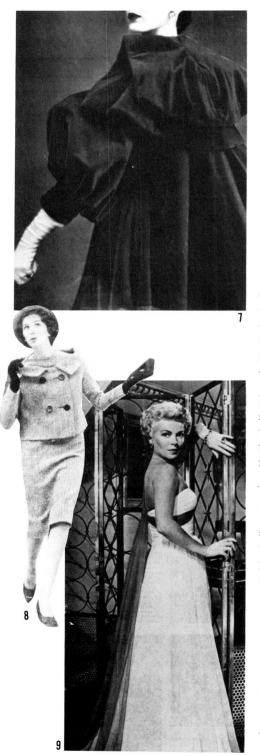

calf). *Barbie's Midi Magic* (1968), *Midi Marvelous* (1968) and *Midi Mood* (1971) show her willingness to compromise!

Women either wore the mini/micro, compromised with the midi, or avoided the whole skirt length controversy with the pantsuit. *Barbie* once again mirrored this alternative, wearing such fashions as *In Stitches* (1971) and *Best Buy Fashions* #867 and #3208.

By the late 1960s, the teenagers who had drawn attention to the problems and needs of their age group were in their early twenties. As their rebellion lost its bite, the fashion mood changed.

The new mood was that of individuality, as seen in the fashions of the Seventies. Unlike the 1960s, individuality did not mean the adoption of a complete look (which was itself individual), but rather a personal style of dressing.

The uncertainty of the early 1970s led, for some people, to a return to a simpler life-style. Two social trends which affected fashion were the back to nature revival and the increasing impact of the women's movement.

---

7. The Balenciaga coat with enormous sweep, melon sleeves and white gloves was the inspiration for *Barbie's* most popular outerwear ensemble, *Red Flair* (1962).

8. The "original" *Career Girl* by Balenciaga.

9. Before Jacqueline Kennedy, fashion influence was exerted by movie stars and costume designers. Here Lana Turner models a "*Barbie*-like" gown designed by Jean Louis for the film *Imitation of Life* (1959).

In fashion, the shape of the body was once again emphasized by the treatment of clothes covering it, as in the Fifties, rather than by the amount of clothing that had been stripped away, as seen in the Sixties. When garments were not knitted to cling, they were cut to reveal the shape beneath. The early 1970s saw the gradual lengthening of skirts and the acceptance of pants for women, which were no longer considered unladylike. "The wider the better!" was the slacks fashion statement. One would not be caught dead in tight, straight-leg pants, quite the contrary by the end of the decade. Bell-bottoms were "it," and *Barbie* had her share of them in *Night Lighter* (1971), *Zig-Zag Bag* (1971), *Pants-Perfect Purple* (1972) and the 1970 classic, *Mood Matchers*.

The maxi coat was the early Seventies fashion sensation. *Barbie* ensembles such as *Maxi 'N Mini* (1970), *Magnificent Midi* (1971) and *Madras Mad* (1972) showed this new style. *Barbie* modeled the popular "prairie look" in such outfits as *Peasant Dressy* (1972) and *Pleasantly Peasanty* (1972).

The "gaucho" was another popular pant style in the 1970s, and *Barbie's Groovin' Gauchos* (1971) and *Gaucho Gear* (1971) mirrored the mid-calf pant craze.

Fringe was a hot detail and could be seen on everything in such fringed fashions as *Fiery Felt* (1970), *Turtle 'N Tights* (1971), *All About Plaid* (1971) and *Fringe Benefits* (1971).

The signature fabric of the Seventies was denim. Fashion designers, Calvin Klein, Gloria Vanderbilt and a host of others capitalized on this as well as *Barbie*. Denim was used from the early 1970s overall craze, *Overall Denim* (1972), to the current designer jeans trend, *Fashion Jeans Barbie* (1983).

The disco craze of the late Seventies brought sequins, spiked heels, Danskins, and three-piece white suits into the spotlight. 1977s *Superstar Barbie* and *Superstar Fashions* exuded the shimmer and shine of this beat-throbbing period.

Fashion in the 1980s saw a rebirth of the dying haute couture. Designer names like Yves Saint Laurent, Calvin Klein and Ralph Lauren became household words. Dressing up was once again sophisticated, elegant and never more carefully executed. Nolan Miller exemplified this with his glamour dressing of his "Dynasty" stars, Linda Evans and Joan Collins. Suddenly a woman could never be surrounded enough by glittering gowns and chic little suits. *Barbie* reflected this in her own Oscar de la Renta designed fashions, complete with furs, sequins and satins.

The popularity of music videos and rock stars like Madonna and

---

10. Echoes of *Barbie's Solo In The Spotlight* (1960) can be seen here in Charles James' black "tulip" gown (1950). The similarity between the two is amazing!

11

Wham brought lace, neon bright colors and wild hairstyles to the fashion world in a new way. *Barbie and The Rockers* show this "hot" new look in dressing.

As the next decade looms closer, one can only guess what the fashion trends will be. Designers are projecting that short, very short hemlines will once again dominate the scene. Be it that or some other fashion style, there is no doubt that *Barbie* will be at the forefront, mirroring the newest look!

12

13

11. The "original" *Enchanted Evening* (1960) is seen here on a 1949 cover of *Vogue* magazine. This timeless creation is by Castillo.

12. In the early 1960s, Jackie Kennedy was the new clothes-conscious heroine and idealized by women everywhere. She made Balenciaga's "pillbox" famous as well as the bouffant coiffure known as the "bubble-cut."

13. During Jackie's "reign," ball gowns were very popular, be they ruffled, caped or bowed! Here *Barbie* models *Debutante Ball* (1966), one of her many ball gowns of the period.

14. The 1960s super model, Jean Shrimpton, dons the rebellious 1965 miniskirt. Skirt length was a provocative statement for women, as hair length was for men.

15. The fashion establishment, which was never too keen on the mini craze, fought back. The solution was the "midi" (middle of the calf) as seen and heard in this ad.

16. Diane Baker and "Tippi" Hedren, looking very *Midge* and *Barbie* in this 1964 Alfred Hitchock movie, *Marnie*. (Yes, that *is* Sean Connery!) *Movie Star News* photograph.

Designers say,"What goes up must come down..."

17. During the late 1960s women wore the mini or the midi. *Barbie* mirrors this choice wearing *Rare Pair* (1970) and *Midi Magic* (1969).

18. Fashion in the early 1970s saw the acceptance of pants for women, no longer considered unladylike. Bell-bottom slacks were "it," and *Barbie* reflects this wearing 1970s *Lemon Kick!*

19. Fringe was a hot 70s detail and could be seen on everything like scarfs, sleeves, boots and, of course, hems, as seen here.

20. *Barbie* models the popular "prairie look" of the early 1970s. The back to nature revival inspired this type of dressing.

21. Designer Calvin Klein was one of the many designers who capitalized on the use of denim — the signature fabric of the 1970s. Designer jeans were a hot fashion trend of the late 70s and still are today!

Fashion Jeans Barbie

Barbie brand boots · Barbie on the pocket · Barbie signature sweater

22

We girls can do anything— *right. Oscar de la Ren* *Right, Bar*

23

Designed by **BILLY BOY**
internationally famous designer!

Feelin' Groovy

Barbie
Limited Edition

Glamour a-go-go! Gift Set
Complete with designer jewelry and lots of fab accessories!

24

22. *Fashion Jeans Barbie* was a result of the late 1970s and current designer jeans trend. The early 1980s saw society, at large, very "label" conscious as *Barbie* clearly shows with her brand boots, logo pocket and signature sweater.

23. Fashion in the 1980s saw a rebirth of the dying haute couture and clothing was once again sophisticated, elegant and never more carefully executed. *Barbie* reflects this in her own Oscar de la Renta designed fashions.

24. *Feelin' Groovy Barbie*, an exciting department store special for 1987 designed by Billy Boy, a long time fan of *Barbie*. This spectacular doll answers the need of the collector to have a quality doll. The 1960s fashion influence can be readily seen in this doll. Interestingly, Billy Boy has projected his own identity on the doll, the way *Barbie* was originally intended.

II. The Birth Of Barbie®

The registered trademarks, the trademarks and the copyrights appearing in italics within this chapter belong to Mattel, Inc., unless otherwise noted.

The late 1950s saw many cultural and social changes. "Rock and Roll," which was to liberate teenagers from the established music, was really in a downslide. Pop music had declined so much that by 1961, Lawrence Welk had a top ten hit in "Calcutta". The late 1950s saw Elvis in the army, Little Richard found God, Buddy Holly was dead, and payola scandals rocked the industry. Teenagers began to look inward to themselves for excitement and adventure. TV shows such as "American Bandstand" with host Dick Clark, and filmed live every day in Philadelphia, (THE dance capital of the US), created "stars" out of ordinary teenagers. In fact, it was the ordinary "teen" herself that was the biggest star to the younger set coming up.

Baby boom children, now around eight years old in 1959, were desperate to grow up. Role models abounded for them to follow. 1959 saw movie producer Ross Hunter bring couture to the screen with the lovely Jean Louis gowns on Lana Turner in *Imitation of Life*. More important, however, was the introduction in this movie of Sandra Dee to the American public. Before the 1960s was even half over,

25. The number one *Barbie*, identified by her pale skin, arched eyebrows, white irises and holes in her feet. This doll is a *Dressed Display Doll*, available only to retailers in the box shown in *Illustration 26*.

26. The rare pink silhouette box with a "TM" label. This box was for Mattel to send store display dolls to the merchant. The "TM" means that *Barbie's* patent was only trademarked and not registered yet. These are the rarest dolls in *Barbie's* world.

millions of teenagers would pattern their lives after what appeared to them to be the perfect teenage girl.

All this seemed a bit overwhelming, if not downright frightening, to the eight-year-olds of 1959. Never before had it been necessary for the "ordinary" teenager to be so fashionable, so sophisticated, so ..."popular." Before, only movie stars needed to be like that. Children were fearful of not being able to live up to the expectations of teendom. A young girl of 13 suddenly found herself out of the tree house and into a crinoline, expected almost overnight to become like the teenage girls that haunted the popular television shows of the day such as "The Donna Reed Show" and "Father Knows Best."

Free from worry about survival like no other generation, this group of children wanted and expected their teenage years to be perfect. To accomplish this, a lot of "training" would be required. This training would have to begin early if on that magic "lucky 13" day, a young girl could make the transition.

Dolls had taken quite a turn over the past five years, as the high heel fashion doll became the staple of the doll market. What was missing from all these dolls, however, was a personality; a life-style that a girl could look up to and strive to achieve. This "personality" had to be successful without being too aggressive; pretty, but not aware of that beauty; popular, but only because she was so nice; and intelligent, but not show-offy. It was a tough package!

In 1959, Mattel was headed by a very imaginative couple, Ruth and Elliot Handler. The pair, along with a partner, Harold Matson, had founded MATTEL (MATT for Matson, EL for Elliot) in 1945. By 1946, profits were

27. 1959 announcement about *Barbie* **in** *Toys and Novelties,* **March 1959, issue. Billed as a "shapely teenage fashion model,"** *Barbie* **was not well received!**

an astonishing $30,000! The Handlers bought out Matson and went on to produce imaginative, quality toys.

The Handler's daughter, Barbara, was herself a boom child, and very much the typical little girl. She often complained to her mother that the paper dolls and fashion dolls she played with were simply not very exciting. Ruth conspired with her to make the "ultimate" fashion doll.

Things always moved fast for the Handlers and by Toy Fair, in February of 1959, they were ready with BARBIE...TEEN-AGE FASHION MODEL. The "original" doll was quite shocking to all who viewed her. Her face featured sharp, penciled-on eyebrows, and her eyes were slanted with white irises. Her very pointed features, made even more stark by her ponytailed hairstyle, seemed eerie. Also disconcerting were her large breasts which seemed a bit out of proportion to her body, which ended with long, tapered legs. Her feet were molded to fit a very high heel open toe shoe, and she came on a round, black pedestal stand that made her seem regal, but unearthly. About as far from all-American as you could get, the first Barbie doll, especially the brunettes, looked much like a person of mixed race.

What there WAS, however, was a wardrobe. It was this wardrobe, perfect in every detail, that sold the doll. Real satin linings in fluffy coats, couture inspired gowns and a wardrobe fit for every occasion began to shape a life-style for Barbie as a globe trotting fashion model that still enjoyed fun. No specific personality was established by Ruth Handler for Barbie. She thought the child should project her own hopes and dreams on the doll and see her own face superimposed on the blank face of Barbie.

28. Young girls of the late 1950s were the new baby boom teenagers such as Eleanor Donohue and Lauren Chapin of "Father Knows Best." Movie Star News photograph.

29. Number one Barbie **as sold to the public. Her feet had holes that fit onto prongs on a round plastic stand. This doll is mint in the box and very hard to find today.**

28

29

Undaunted, the Handlers made their smartest move. A new show, "The Mickey Mouse Club," was a Disney-produced show that featured talented children, many on the brink of "teendom." The afternoon television show was a smash hit with the boom children who viewed many of the characters, especially the older Annette Funicello, as the role model to "bridge" the gap for them between childhood and the teen years.

It is doubtful that the Handlers themselves knew the audience they were playing to when they agreed to sponsor "The Mickey Mouse Club" in 1959. The move gave them a chance to introduce *Barbie* directly to the consumer. The children loved her. Desperate to find just such a doll (like Barbara Handler was), America's children reached for the brass ring of teendom that *Barbie* offered.

By the end of 1959, dealers regretted enormously not ordering heavily on the new fashion doll, for *Barbie* had caught on where it counted ...with the child.

Refinements still had to be made. Elliot Handler said in a personal inter-

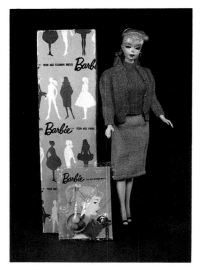

The buyers were not pleased. The doll lacked the all-American look that was popular. Larger dolls were the rage anyway, and there were plenty of other fashion dolls available for a child to play "dress-up" with.

---

30. March 1960, *Toys and Novelties* ad showed *Barbie* back for another great year. Available now were store displays and gift sets. The rich artwork on the packaging was yet to come. 31. A rare number two *Barbie* in a dressed display box. The number two doll is the same as the number one, except she has no holes in her feet. The stand is still round, but held under her arms with a black wire. The fashion is *Sweater Girl*. 32. 1960 *Mix 'N' Match Gift Set*. This set contained several incomplete *Barbie* outfits. The doll shown is a number five doll, already on the market by late 1960.

view with me in February 1987, that the first style *Barbie* head was made by the Japanese factory he had hired without much supervision. In an effort to cut costs, they had gone ahead with the doll. It became apparent in a short time that many parents, fresh from the Pacific theatre of World War II, did not take kindly to *Barbie's* Oriental appearance. It was just too soon. Ruth redesigned the doll, eliminating the costly holes in the feet and pronged stand, and gave *Barbie* smoother eyebrows and big blue eyes. Her makeup still remained that of a fashion model; the blood red lips and nails stood out starkly against her white skin, but this new *Barbie*, in the stores by late 1960, met her requirements.

Eager little girls clamored for the doll in droves. The basic doll sold for $3.00, and came with a black and white striped strapless swimsuit, gold hoop earrings, sunglasses and a round pedestal "to keep her on her feet at fashion shows." This early *Barbie* seemed down to earth enough not to be threatening, but glamorous enough to build dreams on. Just like Sandra Dee, this doll seemed to capture the soul of American teenagers without really trying.

The company catalog of 1959 told of Ruth Handler's philosophy about *Barbie*. "Her clothes really fit! Feminine Magic! A vertible fashion show and every girl can be the star!" Even the names of the outfits such as *Evening Splendour, Gay Parisienne, Cruise Stripe Dress* and *Roman Holiday Separates* describes the envious life-style that *Barbie* represented. Still, the little girl could CONTROL *Barbie* just by

33

34

35

33. Rare 1960 *Party Set* again with incomplete whole outfits. The doll was a number four *Barbie*. 34. Sandra Dee, THE teenager of the early 1960s. Millions wanted to be just like her! *Movie Star News photograph*. 35. By mid 1960, *Barbie's* face had been made to look more all-American. Her eyes were now blue and her eyebrows were curved. This is the number three *Barbie*, exactly as sold.

36

37

holding her in her hand! The future and its many threats seemed a bit less scary and more like something to look very forward to!

The success of *Barbie* in 1959 allowed Mattel, i.e. the Handlers, to rev up introductions. In what would be the first of many well timed moves, Ruth and Elliot got *Barbie* in the limelight by inventing imaginative store displays that would "catch" the eye of both parent and child right in the toy department. These store displays, a relatively new concept, acted as a permanent "salesperson," always on duty to display the items to their best advantage.

The first such display was a lovely cardboard stand that contained six plastic cylinders into which a retailer could slip a *Barbie* doll already dressed in an outfit. The background of the display used glamorous portrait shots of other *Barbie* dolls wearing the rest of the fashions available in 1960. It was a brilliant marketing strategy, and one that would propel the Handlers and Mattel into fame and fortune.

Adding to collecting history, Mattel shipped the retailer the dressed

36. The *Barbie* fashions were what sold the doll. Never had a doll owned such a wardrobe! Shown here is *Commuter Set*, illustrated only in the first three booklets.

37. A number three *Barbie* wears *Commuter Set*!

dolls in pink boxes with silhouettes of *Barbie* on them. The idea was once the display was outdated or an outfit discontinued, this box could be used to sell the doll. Most, if not all, retailers discarded these boxes when placing the dolls in the displays, making them a valuable collectible.

Also issued in 1960 were the first of many gift sets with names like *Party*

38. Shown only in the first booklet, a number one *Barbie* wears *Gay Parisienne*.

39. Another early fashion, *Roman Holiday Separates*, shown on a number two *Barbie*.

40. *Easter Parade*, one of the rare early fashions, shown on a number three *Barbie*.

Set, *Mix 'N' Match Set* and *Trousseau Set*. These did not as yet have artwork on them for the identity of *Barbie* was still that of the child, but they contained a doll surrounded by several lovely complete outfits, or in some cases, incomplete parts to mix together.

By the end of 1960, a total of three dolls would have been tried and changed. The first, with her holes in her feet for the pronged stand and her white eyes was rapidly discontinued. The second, with the same head, only no holes in the feet, still was the wrong face. A third, that had the American look with blue eyes, but still the white skin tones, lasted slightly longer.

With the introduction of the number four *Barbie* in late 1960, with her lifelike flesh tones, Mattel had made *Barbie* a household word. Scarcely was a child alive that did not own or at least want a *Barbie* doll. *Barbie* was helping an entire nation of preteens grow up!

The *Barbie* era was about to begin...

III. The Early Years Of Barbie® Fashions (1959-1963)

The registered trademarks, the trademarks and the copyrights appearing in italics within this chapter belong to Mattel, Inc., unless otherwise noted.

The beginning of 1960 marked the start of a new era in America. An interesting contrast existed between the "adult" culture and teenage values. In 1960, the top three rated television shows were "Gunsmoke," "Wagon Train" and "Have Gun, Will Travel." Clearly, adults were not as interested in glamour and broken hearts as were teenagers. At the same time, the song "Teen Angel," by Mark Dinning was breaking hearts and the charts with the story of a young love that ended in tragedy. The Sandra Dee, Troy Donahue-type of love was what the young wanted. Soon, they would have it!

As mentioned in the last chapter, many collectors believe that the number four Barbie, with her new flesh tones, actually was the "original" Barbie. Now that the creation of Barbie was settled and she was selling briskly, she needed some sort of an identity.

Ruth Handler's son's name was Ken. In 1960, it was decided to use that name and create a boyfriend for Barbie. At Toy Fair, 1961, Ken...He's a Doll was introduced. The play on words was brilliant, as the slang "doll" was a word describing a cute teenage boy.

Ken was the perfect "boy next door" type of companion for Barbie.

Just looking at him, a mother knew her daughter was safe. An entire wardrobe of "activity" fashions was created for Ken that ranged from tennis gear to pajamas.

I cannot resist the urge to say that at Barbie doll conventions and doll shows in general, I am often overwhelmed by the number of men who had Ken dolls as a child. I did, and remember at the time loving the idea of having an idol to look up to, much the way little girls did Barbie. I did not then, nor do today, understand why a little boy should be denied such "friends." Thankfully, many boys are sharing love with dolls today, as boy's "companion" dolls, and Cabbage Patch Kids dolls are often seen in their arms. My entire love of dolls today as an adult is based on my wonderful shared experiences with my Ken doll!

41. The exciting new "bubble cut," on Barbie, wearing Solo in the Spotlight! This was one of Barbie's most famous outfits!

Cabbage Patch Kids® is a registered trademark of Coleco Industries, Inc.,

42

By 1961, the world of *Barbie* was moving ahead. A popular television show that year was "Hawaiian Eye," and featured a lovely young *Barbie*-type, Connie Stevens, as Cricket Blake. Cricket still had her long blonde pony-tail, but the entire front of her hair had been layered into a new style, the bubble cut. Teens everywhere began copying her hairstyle, and many took the plunge and removed the long back. Mattel responded by issuing *Barbie* in the new *Bubble Cut* version. The lips were still red and really nothing was different except the hairstyle. Starting with the ponytail dolls this year, a new material, Saran, was used for the entire ponytail head including the bangs. This firmer banged doll is considered

42. A number three *Barbie* models *Busy Gal*. Not only was *Barbie* a top fashion model, but obviously a talented designer of these fashions, as well!

43. 1961 saw the addition of redheads to the line. Officially called "Titian," the color was that of the real life *Barbie*, Barbara Handler. These dolls were made at the ratio of 1 to 100 blondes, and are today quite rare.

44. The new 1961 *Bubble Cut Barbie* and the ponytail *Barbie* of that year. The dolls were identical except for the hairstyle.

43

the number five *Barbie*. It is at this point that the numbering stops. After this, so many changes in lip color and hairstyling existed that numbering would be impossible. Also new in 1961 was the addition of redheads to the line. Ruth Handler had a special place for red or "titian" haired dolls, for the real life *Barbie* had this color hair!

In 1962, Ken became a sturdier doll. The 1961 version had a type of molded head with "flocked-on" hair. It looked wonderful, (just like a crew cut), but when it got wet, the flocking came right off.

This new 1962 Ken had hair molded in the new "butch" cut. This style left a longer strip of hair along the front of the head that was pushed up every morning with a "butch" wax stick! Girls were not alone in their obsession with hair!

Fashion was changing and so was makeup. Teen girls now were tiring of the blood red lips popular in the late 1950s. Paler lips and softer eye makeup was the new "in" thing. *Barbie* reflected this in 1962 with lips in varying shades.

Many long-time buyers of *Barbie* remember, like I do, of seeing a friend have a particular doll, and then going to the store to find it! There were endless variations, just like there are today with *Cabbage Patch Kids*. My young experience was to sit there and pull down doll after doll, lifting the lid of the box, until the store employees finally politely asked me to leave! In fact, a close friend of mine had a doll that was an ordinary blonde bubble, but with white lips, that I did not see again for 25 years, when I finally found one at a local show! Many collectors are not aware of just how mass-manufactured and how different these dolls were. By 1961, over six million *Barbie* dolls a year were pro-

45

46

45. In 1961, *Barbie* got a new hairstyle and a boyfriend, *Ken, He's a Doll!* The resemblance to real people is astonishing, as in this record cover by Paul and Paula.

46. A number five ponytail *Barbie* and *Ken* model *Registered Nurse* and *Dr. Ken*. Of course, *Barbie* had to be the nurse. It would be 20 years before *Barbie* would get a doctor's uniform and diploma!

47. Troy Donahue seems to exemplify the *Ken* look! In this photograph he is even wearing *Ken's* outfit, *Time for Tennis! Movie Star News photograph.*

48. The lovely Diane Baker, shown in this 1961 publicity photograph, was the epitome of *Bubble Cut Barbie!* She would go on to change her hairstyle exactly to what *Barbie* would wear in 1964! *Movie Star News photograph.*

47

48

49. Very collectible items from this period are the *Dressed Box Dolls*. The boxes were "banded" to identify them. Shown are *Tennis Anyone* on *Barbie* and *Time for Tennis* on *Ken*.

50. The adventures of *Barbie* and *Ken* were so exciting to youngsters that gradually distinct personalities evolved for *Barbie*. Dell comics published an entire series of comics that depicted their lives in teenage splendor!

49

50

duced. This is the reason why out-of-box dolls from this period are not worth much. Every little girl alive had one or more *Barbie* dolls and many have survived in excellent condition.

By 1963, dazzling artwork on the *Barbie* packaging told the story of a beautiful girl's wonderful life almost as well as the dolls themselves.

Ruth Handler was being urged more and more to establish a personality for *Barbie*, something that she rebelled against.

As a compromise, the line was expanded. A new doll, *Fashion Queen Barbie*, was issued that consisted of a molded head and three very high style wigs. There was a redhead "flip" inspired by Shelley Fabares of "The Donna Reed Show," a white or platinum "bubble on bubble," and a Cleopatra style of a brunette "page boy." There was still lots of choice for a little girl. *Barbie* could be a projection of the child's identity as Ruth Handler

wanted, or have her own personality. It was hard for *Barbie* not to have a personality when she had a boyfriend, and now a girlfriend, *Midge*!

Midge was the doll that, in my opinion, cemented the idea of a personality for *Barbie*. *Midge* was the perfect best friend. Not envious, but supportive, she was very willing to play a secondary role in *Barbie's* adventures. *Midge* was the type of girl that knew she could not be "Queen of the Prom," but was thrilled to get close to it through her association with *Barbie*.

Random House published a series of novels about *Barbie*, *Ken* and *Midge* that told of their lives in Willows, Wisconsin, a fictional town that could be "Anywhere USA." *Barbie* and the

51. *Barbie* and her new friend, *Midge*! *Midge* was the perfect friend to *Barbie*, and willingly took a supporting role in her adventures. They are wearing *Silken Flame* and *Party Date*.

52. Mint in box vintage dolls. Number one "flocked hair" *Ken*, the new 1962 *Bubble Cut Barbie* in red swimsuit, a "swirl' ponytail *Barbie*, and the second issue of *Ken* with molded hair. Dolls in this condition are worth more than double dolls out of the box.

53. During this period, the Suzy Goose Company made gorgeous furniture for *Barbie*. Shown is a number four *Barbie* in *Nighty Negligee* and *Midge* in *Sweet Dreams*.

54. The accessories for the clothing are the difficult part to locate today. Shown is *Candy Striper Volunteer* for *Barbie* and *Campus Hero* for *Ken*. The little spoons, boxes of tissues and varsity letters are what drive collectors crazy when trying to complete an outfit!

52

53

54

55. *Playthings Magazine* ad for March 1963, saw the addition of *Fashion Queen Barbie* and wigs to the line. The store display shown was available to the retailer. Mattel was one of the first companies to use this method of marketing.

gang attended Willows High; all the beautiful things that happened to *Barbie* just DID. She, like Bill Woggon's *Katy Keene*, was a beautiful, shy, down-to-earth girl that no one could resent.

The life of *Barbie* was an enviable one. A set called *Barbie Baby Sits* was created to concentrate on the "average girl" aspects of *Barbie's* personality. Her link to the world of high fashion was lessening. Most, if not all, of the Mattel licensed products from the period reflect the idea that *Barbie* and *Ken* were just average teenagers that were born leaders. This was an ideal that the television shows of the day aspired to greatly. Even brother teams like Wally and Beaver on "Leave it to Beaver" were children you could be

proud of. There was a satisfaction often missing today in making the honor roll, being a crossing guard, and serving as lunchroom monitor. If, through all this you could be pretty, popular and well-groomed, well, the brass ring was yours. At least this was the dream that was told to the baby boomers. Later on this dream, for some, would turn into a nightmare, especially for some women who would realize that Cinderella was often just a prisoner in a castle. But for now, being "perfect," according to the standards of the day, was a goal all its own.

The *Barbie* fashions of this and the couture period were the best ever made. Zippers that really zipped, tiny charm bracelets and real silk linings gave the clothing a tailored look that

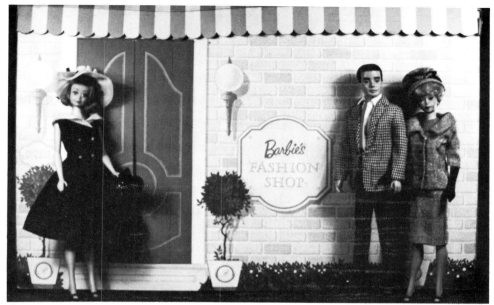

56

56. Naturally a fashion model had to have a place to model her fashions. This *Fashion Shop* was a clever cardboard shop for *Barbie*. *Midge* waits at the model's entrance in *After Five*. *Ken* is the escort in *Country Clubin'* and *Barbie* models *Career Girl*.

57. Inside the *Fashion Shop*, *Midge* models *Senior Prom* and *Barbie* wears *Sophisticated Lady*.

57

58. Irwin Plastics in New York had the license for many clever *Barbie* accessories. Shown are *Barbie* in *Resort Set* going sailing with *Ken* in *The Yachtsman!*

59. *Barbie* got a little sister, *Skipper*®, in 1964. The "family" concept was expanding, as was the imaginative themes for outfits such as these masquerade costumes.

today is viewed as magical. The tiny garments are so perfectly made that if enlarged, they would suffice even the fussiest of dressers. Adding to the appeal of every *Barbie* outfit was a label identifying it as a genuine *Barbie* fashion, and obviously of superior quality. Tiny velvet lined purses, white tricot gloves and the perfect footwear for each ensemble added to the mystique of these outfits. Other companies tried to copy Mattel's style. In fact, *Barbie* was and is the most imitated fashion doll in history. The truth is that nothing ever came close and probably never will in terms of fashion quality and theme selection.

The outfits were assigned a stock number, in the early period a 900 series number. This was not to aid the child or the collector, but for the merchant to identify and inventory his

stock. For this reason they have been omitted from the text and illustrations as often they are not continuous and can be confusing.

There is one thing for certain. By 1964, *Barbie* was the dominating force in the toy industry. In order to retain that title, many revisions would have to take place. Teenagers were on a roller coaster ride of fads and fancies. Could *Barbie* remain "Queen of the Prom" in the toy world?

We already know the answer to that astounding question. *Barbie* did go on to the couture period, a period inspired by a great lady, Jacqueline Kennedy. Just ahead for *Barbie* was college and a more "mature" way of dressing. The boom children were growing up and so was *Barbie*!

60. Spectacular gift sets were available during the early 1960s, such as this *On Parade* set. It is very rare to find these sets unopened today. They are valued at well over $500 each when in this condition.

61. Available for *Barbie* were many *Paks*, or cheaper separate pieces for outfits. This rare set called *Mix 'N' Match* shows *Barbie* and her many *Pak* fashions.

62. *Barbie* shows her versatility in this *Round the Clock Gift Set.* Outfits are *Career Girl, Fancy Free* and *Senior Prom* with the addition of a fur stole!

63. *Barbie* and *Ken* wearing *Open Road* and *Rally Day,* go for a spin in Irwin Plastic's *Ken's Hot Rod!*

64. *Barbie* in *Enchanted Evening*, one of the all-time favorite outfits, escorted by *Ken* in *Tuxedo*. Playing the rare Suzy Goose Piano is *Allan, Ken's Buddy* wearing *Best Man*.

65. *Skipper* got a new friend, *Skooter*, in 1965, but she looks so good in *Red Sensation*, I had to use her! *Fashion Queen Barbie* models *Sheath Sensation*.

66. Teenage life is depicted with uncanny reality in *Barbie* outfits and accessories. Here in the *Campus Sweet Shoppe, Barbie* wears *Friday Night Date, Ken* sports *Dreamboat, Allan* is wearing *Play Ball* and *Midge* rests in *Pak* separates.

67. The richness of the lavish fashions is seen here in *Midge* wearing *It's Cold Outside*, in the rare red version, *Barbie* shows off *Red Flair* (the longest running outfit of the early period) and *Skipper* looks lovely in *Dress Coat*.

68. Millions of children acted out teenage life with their dolls. The clever themes of the fashions allowed realistic play. Shown are *Ken* in *Fun on Ice*, *Barbie* in *Ice Breaker* and *Skipper* in *Skating Fun*.

69. The winter fun possibilities were endless for *Barbie* and the gang. *Barbie* is wearing *Ski Queen*, *Ken* in *Ski Champion*, *Skipper* is in *Sleddin' Fun* and *Midge* models *Winter Holiday*.

70

71

72

70. Whitman made lovely paper dolls of *Barbie* and *Midge* during the early years. The personality of the two girls can be readily seen. These, uncut, are worth $25 each.

71. Afraid to make *Barbie* too sophisticated, Mattel toned down her high fashion image. *Barbie* was a down-to-earth girl who baby sat, as in *Barbie Baby-Sits*, and had a pet dog, shown in *Dog & Duds*.

72. Drive-ins were popular with teens in the early 1960s. Shown in Irwin Plastics *Barbie's Car* are *Barbie* in *Movie Date*, *Ken*, *Midge* and *Allan* wear *Pak* fashions. The backdrop is a lovely scene from *Barbie Goes to College*.

73. The easygoing teenage life depicted in *Ken* wearing *Sailor, Barbie* in *Garden Party, Midge* in *Let's Dance* and *Allan* in *Army Air Force*. It was still patriotic to depict sterotypical roles for teens.

74. Frivolous fun for *Barbie* and *Midge* in *Suburban Shopper* in blue and *Busy Morning* in red! The tiny dial phones and decorated purses are hard-to-find accessories today.

75. Serious careers were depicted for *Barbie* and *Ken* such as *Barbie* in *American Airlines Stewardess* and *Ken's American Airlines Pilot*. Teenagers were growing up and so was *Barbie!*

75

IV.
The Couture Period (1964-1966)

The registered trademarks, the trademarks and the copyrights appearing in italics within this chapter belong to Mattel, Inc., unless otherwise noted

As mentioned previously, the baby boomers were growing up. Many, by 1964, were graduating from high school, and were on their way to college. Never had so many from one generation gone on for higher education. A "liberal arts" degree (bascially meaning you were versed somewhat in ALL areas), was the "American Dream." Later, only those with highly specialized skills would be employable, but for now, just having a college degree would be enough. Many high schools boasted that up to 90% of their graduates went on to college, and often this became the focal point of education.

The next generation coming up was faced with a more mature role model. The James Dean and Natalie Wood-type of the late 1950s teen had learned that reckless fun was too costly. The Sandra Dee, Troy Donahue crowd were getting married! Younger preteens found themselves looking to older women such as America's First Lady, Jacqueline Kennedy, and later, Lady-bird Johnson. Even the top rated television show of 1964, "Bewitched," starred an older, married woman, Elizabeth Montgomery.

If one had to name an influence on fashion for the beginning of the decade,

it would have to be Jacqueline Kennedy. Born into aristocracy, she was the closest to a queen this country ever had. Columnists delighted in listing her ensembles on the society pages; designers were glad to be designing for women instead of teenagers.

In 1964, Mattel made the decision to allow *Barbie* to grow up. Graduation outfits were available, and a set, *Barbie Goes to College*, with a dorm room for *Barbie* and *Midge* replaced the *Dream House* of *Barbie's* high school years.

The women's movement was just getting under way. Along the road to the "American Dream," women were realizing that they, too, had more to offer society than dirty diapers. As women attended colleges and universities in record numbers, they became aware of just how they had been shortchanged by society, as far back in this country as the Constitution, which did not even allow them basic human rights such as voting. They wanted and got more. Change was the password of this period.

76. The new "American Girl" *Barbie* (with lifelike bendable legs), wears White House inspired, *Fashion Luncheon.*

77. The back of the *Fashion Queen Barbie* box told the beautiful story of a fashion model's life. By now, the identity of *Barbie* was well established.

78. A lavish gift set featuring *Fashion Queen Barbie, Ken* and their trousseau was on the market during this period. Unbelievably rare today, it brings, unopened, over $700!

79. *The Wedding Party Gift Set* allowed for fantasy play about the wedding of *Barbie* and *Ken*. Officially, they have never been married to this day!

80. Friends of *Barbie* and *Ken*, as these shown in perfect as new condition, expanded play possibilities and taught children about relationships among friends. From left, *Ricky, Midge, Allan* and *Skooter.*

81. *Barbie* and *Ken* graduated from high school in 1964 and, of course, went on to State "U."

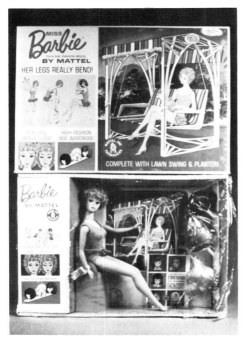

82. In 1964, Mattel issued *Miss Barbie*. She was the only doll issued with a hard plastic head and sleep eyes. Goulish in appearance, she was rapidly discontinued, leaving an outstanding, but bizarre collectible.

83. *Barbie* was the perfect college student. Naturally, her modeling experience led to acting. In her *Little Theatre*, she, *Ken* and *Midge* act out the timeless drama of *Cinderella*.

Mattel felt that the next group of youngsters would like to see *Barbie* as a career woman. Her relationship with her high school sweetheart, *Ken* did not lead to marriage and babies, (much to the concern of many moralists of the day), but to various "careers." During this period *Barbie* became an art critic, as well as an artist, a student teacher, a fashion editor, an entertainer, an actress in little theatre, a world traveler, and still retained her interest in modeling!

Barbie excelled at college just as she did in high school. As a sorority sister, homecoming queen and cheerleader, she was second to none!

Little girls had tamed down a bit from their desire to grow up; to satisfy this need to play with an alter ego, Mattel issued *Skipper*. She, along with *Ken*, would remain at *Barbie's* side for the next 28 years. Billed as *Barbie's Little Sister*, *Skipper* had matching "junior-edition" size fashions that corresponded to *Barbie's*. The same care and workmanship went into *Skipper* as did *Barbie*. Her clothing and her life-style was spelled out to the buyer on the wonderfully designed packaging of the period. Like *Midge*, *Skipper* was willing to play a supportive role, but you knew by the twinkle in her eye that some day she would come close herself to being like *Barbie*.

Trapped in pertpetual puberty, *Skipper* throughout the years has remained loyal to all of *Barbie's* dreams and ideas, never forsaking them for her own.

Experimentation abounded at Mattel in 1964. *Midge* got a new boyfriend in *Allan*. Billed as *Ken's Buddy*, it was a natural foursome. *Allan* was just like *Midge* in that he was loyal to *Ken*, and acknowledged that there was nothing wrong in being either the leader or the follower, if one

84

85

84. Foreign travel as an exchange student was necessary for all college bound boom children. Here *Midge* and *Allan* visit Holland, while *Barbie* and *Ken* return from Mexico. Other *Travel Outfits* included a pair of Swiss outfits, a pair of Hawaiian togs and a kimono for *Barbie*.

85. The big news of 1965 was "Lifelike Bendable Legs." The dolls were all updated to a "preppie" image that would last only two years. Notice the shy look for *Ken* this year!

was content in the role. This was a valuable lesson and one that is often forgotten today. Without Indians, there could be no chiefs! 1980s parents tend to push all of their children into leadership, when many would make wonderful, happy followers. The end result is often disasterous. *Ken*, and his relationship with *Allan*, taught many little girls (and boys) lessons of life they could not have learned elsewhere.

86. A new hairstyle, nicknamed "The American Girl," arrived with a bang. Featuring one length sides and back ("blunt" cut), and flirty bangs, it would later resurface in 1981 as Linda Evans' signature hairstyle! Here movie actress Yvonne Craig, ("Batgirl") shows off her new "do." *Movie Star News* photograph.

87. *Jack and Jill* magazine often ran ads for *Barbie* dolls. Note the "American Girl" hairdo on the mother in this 1965 ad.

88. The couture period at its high fashion best shown here in *Gold 'N Glamour* (1965), *On the Avenue* (1965) and *Saturday Matinee* (1965).

Many other doll companies were using innovative ideas that were spawned of the post war prosperity. Mattel, eager to retain *Barbie's* crown, issued a *Miss Barbie*, which had a sleep eye feature and hard plastic head. If ever a doll had no personality, this was it! Bland, and almost goulish, it rapidly faded from view, but left a valuable collectible.

1965 was a big year for *Barbie*. This year she and her friends got "bendable legs." This feature was wonderful, and allowed the dolls to pose realistically. The technology was very advanced, for a knee joint was inside the leg, and from the outside could not be seen. Billed as "lifelike," it certainly gave new dimension to the dolls.

Also new in 1965 was a hairstyle for *Barbie* called the "American Girl." Basically a chin length blunt cut with bangs, it was more youthful than the teased bubble cuts. This style also

89. *Barbie* and *Ken* pose for prom pictures! Both *Kens* are wearing *Tuxedo, Barbie* wears *Fraternity Dance,* (1965) and *Junior Prom* (1965).

90. Different colors of *Barbie's Sweater Girl*, available since 1959, appeared. These are in pink and navy blue.

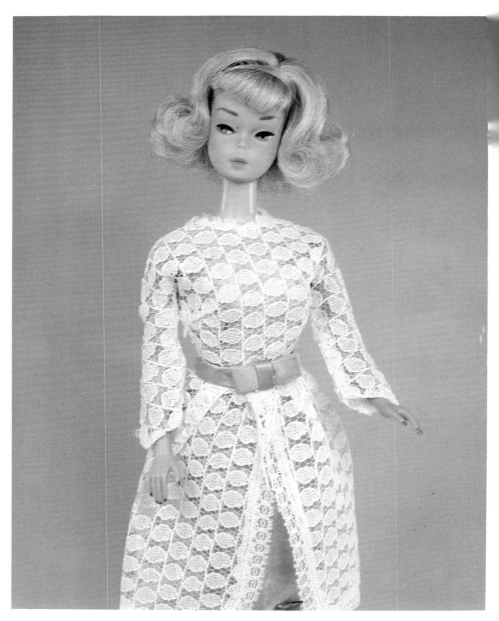

91. A very rare version of the "American Girl" doll is this side-parted flip *Bendable Leg Barbie*. She is wearing *Garden Wedding* (1966). This doll in this condition brings $700 and up even out of the box!

92. Winning awards was part of college life! Here *Barbie* shows off her oil painting skills in *Modern Art* (1965) and *Poodle Parade* (1965). These outfits, made only for one year, and having many accessories, are very difficult to locate complete. (Years are given for these outfits to help the collector see the limited availability.)

93. Hair play was big news in the 1960s. A set called *Color and Curl* was issued that featured a *Fashion Queen Barbie* head and wigs that could be cut, colored and curled. The set works well, as seen in my handiwork for this wig! The doll models *White Magic* (1964) and a *Pak* sheath.

94. The concept of matching outfits for *Barbie* and *Skipper* was continued throughout the period. Here our girls are shipbound in nautical inspired attire. *Barbie* wears *Aboard Ship* (1965) and *Skipper* poses coyly in *Ship Ahoy* (1965).

95. Red, white and black were high fashion colors in the mid 1960s. Here a *Bendable Leg Midge* models *Music Center Matinee* (1966) while *Bendable Leg Barbie* dons *Pretty as a Picture* (1966). Dressed to kill is a flaming redhead *Color Magic Barbie* in *Matinee Fashion* (1965).

96. 1966 saw the introduction of *Color Magic Barbie*. Her hair could change colors with an applied solution that could also change the color of her special outfits. Although mass marketed, she is most difficult to locate today.

97. *Ken* and *Barbie* were BOTH astronauts in 1965, boosting the fledgling woman's movement. Twenty-two years later, *Barbie* would again be a space explorer!

98. Couture period outfits were beautifully made and highly accessorized. Shown are *Barbie's Dancing Doll* (1965) and *Skipper's Me 'N My Doll* (1965). Contained in this set is a tiny *Barbie* doll for *Skipper* to play with!

99. By the mid 1960s, vinyl houses had replaced the cardboard structures of the early period. This house is very unusual and features a typical period living room.

100. The lavish artwork on all *Barbie* accessories told the lifestyle of *Barbie* beautifully. Here *Barbie* is dressed in *Riding in the Park* (1966) and poses with horse *Prancer*.

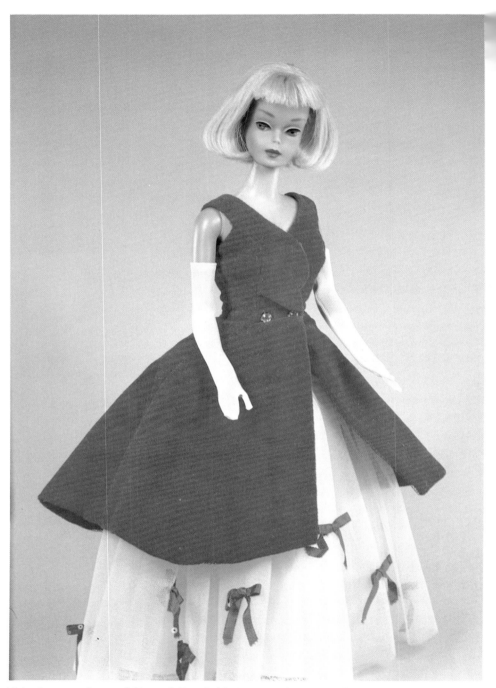

101. A stunning red-lipped *Bendable Leg Barbie* is ready to go on stage in the rare *Benefit Performance* (1966).

heralded the beginnings of long, straight hair that would dominate fashion for the next ten years.

All the "bendable leg" dolls were mass manufactured but today, for some reason, are difficult to locate in original packaging.

Both *Barbie* and *Midge* were available as separate molded heads in a *Color and Curl Set* that featured red and blonde wigs that could be colored and set. Actually, this was the first type of wig or hair on *Barbie* that actually could be "set." The other fibers used had the curl put in at the factory by a heat method and could not be changed. The styling possibilities were endless, and the set worked even better than advertised!

1966 saw this curlable, colorable hair rooted right into the head in *Color Magic Barbie*. This doll added the versatility of real hair play, absent since *Barbie's* birth. The doll is a delight and somewhat difficult to find today in good condition, due to the many "beauty" sessions she undoubtedly had to endure.

Also in 1966 *Skipper* got a new friend, *Skooter*. 1965 saw a little boy, *Ricky*, join the group, and *Skooter* completed the picture. Both had the "follower" type of personality that all of *Barbie's* friends had and would have until *Barbie's Modern Cousin, Francie* arrived later in the year!

Francie is my favorite of all the *Barbie* family dolls, and it is a great temptation to devote an entire chapter to her. The mid 1960s saw the arrival of many British rock stars. The Beatles, already a household word, were taking teens out of the matronly look just

103. Ball gowns abounded during the mid 1960s. *Bendable Leg Barbie* models *Magnificence* (1965). Her companion is a rare brunette *Bendable Leg Midge* in *Debutante Ball* (1966).

recently made popular and into wild, outlandish styles.

Mattel, already quaking with having put *Barbie* into an older, more sophisticated look, was stumped! Would this Mod thing last? What did teenagers want? Board meetings were held and it was decided that for at least another year *Barbie* would be left untouched. To satisfy the Mod type of child, *Francie* would be introduced.

Loosely based on the character Francie Lawrence (Gidget), *Francie* was the epitome of the character played by Sandra Dee in movies and Sally Field on television. *Francie* was smaller than *Barbie*, but her fashions had a "Carnaby Street," London flair. She also featured a new innovation, rooted eyelashes! *Francie* would be so popular that next year *Barbie* would be redesigned to look more youthful, more energetic...more like *Francie*! For the first time *Barbie* was to be a follower. The only saving grace was in the stories about *Barbie* and *Francie* in the *Barbie Magazine* (the official Fan Club publication). *Barbie* was older, and therefore wiser. It still was a year before the Beatles would say, "Never trust anyone over thirty!"

The "family" concept of *Barbie's* world was becoming very enticing. Other dolls such as Remco's *Littlechap Family* and Ideal's *Tammy* and her family necessitated the move to expand the original *Barbie* concept.

1966 also saw the introduction of *Tutti, Barbie and Skipper's Little Sister*, and her twin brother, *Todd*. Smaller than *Skipper*, these little dolls were a

104. From formals to sportswear, *Barbie* had it all. Here they are ready for a camping trip in *Outdoor Life* (1965) and *Vacation Time* (1965). These outfits came with little cameras to photograph the scenery.

105. The end of the couture period saw the last of "traditional" fashions for over a decade. *Barbie* and *Ken* play at marriage in 1966 with *Here Comes the Bride* and *Here Comes the Groom*. These outfits, like the life-style they depict, are rare today! Just ahead was the British Invasion and MOD!

106. *Barbie* takes the loving cup as Prom Queen in 1964 dressed in *Campus Sweetheart* (1964-65). Her moment of triumph is richly illustrated on this board game from the period.

105

107. More fabulous couture gowns! These rare outfits are *Formal Occasion* (1967), *Midnight Blue* (1964) on a rare white lip *Barbie* (remember those AWFUL lipstick colors?) and *Evening Enchantment* (1967).

108. The popularity of "Lurex" gold thread used in period clothing, reflected in couture *Barbie* clothing. Left is *Holiday Dance* (1965), middle is *Golden Glory* (1965), and on the right, *Evening Gala* (1966).

delightful addition to the *Barbie* family. Together, *Barbie, Ken, Midge, Allan, Skipper, Skooter, Ricky, Francie, Tutti* and *Todd* all made up the "American Dream Family" and their friends. The couture period, like President Kennedy's life, was over almost before it began.

Next year, an entire new look for *Barbie*!

---

109. A mid 1960s sorority meeting! A *Wig Wardrobe* molded *Midge* head in a *Color and Curl* wig, wears *Lunch Date* (1964). A blonde *Color Magic Barbie* is telling of her *London Tour* (1966). *Barbie* spins records in *Disc Date* (1965), while another *Barbie* wears the new mini skirt in *Travel Togethers* (1967).

V.
The Mod Scene
(1967-1971)

The registered trademarks, the trademarks and the copyrights appearing in italics within this chapter belong to Mattel, Inc., unless otherwise noted.

1967 was really an important year in pop culture. The "British Invasion" of rock music and clothing styles from England was starting to make even the most conservative teenagers turn more "Mod." Magazines such as *Seventeen, Glamour* and even *Vogue* were leaning more toward "young" fashions instead of the classic, but matronly Jacqueline Kennedy type of dress. "The Motown Sound," using black groups like "The Supremes" were gaining air time in white clubs and radio stations. Cultures were blending as youth forgot about tradition.

It must be pointed out that these influences were NOT just associated with the lower and middle classes. College students from the finest universities also had become "Mod." It was strictly fashion and music FUN!

Barbie, by the start of this period, had really become very high fashion, with the pillbox hat and suit look. With the popularity of *Francie*, and her "Mod" wardrobe, Mattel thought it safe to loosen up *Barbie* and go with the youth movement. Afraid to resurrect the controversy *Barbie* caused in 1959, Mattel moved cautiously.

The real support for *Barbie* being a bit more modern came from the boom children themselves. Annette Funicello, once the "Now It's Time to Say Goodbye" sweetheart of 12 on the "Mickey Mouse Club," had grown up into a busty, sexy young lady! Looking a lot like *Barbie* herself, she still retained innocence in her *Beach Party* movies, as did Sandra Dee earlier in *Gidget*.

Mattel wasted no time. At Toy Fair, 1967, a NEW *Barbie* was introduced. The same size and shape, the big change was her face. Made from a new mold, it mirrored the "growing up young" look that was popular. Available in such hair shades as "Chocolate Bon-Bon" and "Go Go Co-Co," the doll featured the new long straight hair with bangs ("fringe" if you were Mod) and rooted eyelashes! A new advance, a twist and turn waist, made this *Barbie* more posable than ever before.

In May, a huge trade-in program was launched, where a child could bring in an old doll, and for $1.50, receive a brand new one. The dolls were traded in by the millions, with the old dolls given to charity. (This accounts for the scarcity of the number one and number two dolls.) Also available was a standard version of the

110. A *Talking Barbie* from 1968 shows she is MOD in *Fancy-Dancy,* never shown in a fashion booklet, but featured in the Mattel catalog for 1967, fall supplement.

111. A relaxing moment for a 1967 *Twist 'N Turn Barbie* in *Mini-Prints* never shown in any fashion booklet!

112. Even the 1967 paper dolls showed that "*Barbie* Has a New Look!"

113. The 1967 trade-in offer led to the turning in of millions of older dolls. For $1.50 a child could get a new doll in exchange for an old doll.

114. *Barbie Talk* advertisement for the "trade-in" dolls.

115. *Twiggy*, London's top fashion model, joined the Mattel doll family in 1967. She was able to wear all of *Francie's* MOD fashions, as illustrated here wearing *Style Setters*, never shown in any fashion booklet! The *Twiggy* outfit is *Twiggy-Do's*.

116. The Mod influence is shown in *Barbie's Trail-Blazer* outfit from 1967, *Francie's Merry-Go-Rounders* from 1969 and *Skipper's Pink Princess*, 1970.

117. *Barbie's MODern Cousin, Francie* was a major influence on fashion trends. A 1966 straight leg *Francie* is shown modeling 1969 *Land Ho!*

118. 1967 saw *Francie* get a friend, *Casey*. She could wear all the groovy Mod fashions such as *The Yellow Bit* from 1969.

doll with straight non-bendy legs and no eyelashes.

Perhaps the biggest news of 1967 was the introduction of a black version of *Francie*. Identical to the white doll, she was a complete failure. Blacks still longed to buy into the American dream through fantasy. *Barbie* and her family were white and espoused the ideal that EVERYONE, black and white ascribed to. Years later blacks would want the American dream of their own and ethnic dolls would be popular. It was just too soon in 1967.

Barbie's world got many new "friends" that year. *Tutti, Barbie's Little Sister*, appeared in several new play sets that featured well done accessories like swings and stoves. She also got a new playmate, *Chris*. Available in blonde and brunette, *Chris* and *Todd* (*Tutti's* brother) were the junior set.

The favorite new doll of the year was that of *Twiggy*, London's top fashion model. Volumes could be written on the psychology of a scrawny kid with a cockney accent that changed the entire world! *Twiggy*, in doll form, was stunning, with a *Francie*-sized body so they could share Mod fashions.

119. A 1968 *Talking Barbie* models 1969s *Country Capers,* while a 1967 *Twist 'n Turn Barbie* shows off *Fashion Shiner,* of 1967. The matching paper dolls were an art into themselves.

120. The heroes of the baby boomers themselves were growing up! Shelly Fabares, who led many a child into teenage life on "The Donna Reed Show," sported the same hairstyle as *Barbie* in 1967! *Movie Star News photograph.*

121. Even Annette Funicello from the "Mickey Mouse Club" was growing up! Her "Beach Party" type movies were taking "Gidget" another step forward! *Movie Star News photograph.*

Francie, Casey and *Twiggy,* (*Casey* was another American friend of *Francie,* who had short hair in a "Sasson" cut, and wore one dangling triangular gold earring!) went everywhere together. This, again, was fulfilling Ruth Handler's original concept that the choices were many for a child who selected *Barbie* and her world to play with. If the child wanted to grow up glamourous, there was *Barbie.* If she wanted to be the new type of "Mod Teen," there was *Francie*; if the little girl wanted a doll to remind her of herself, there was still *Skipper,* and the even younger *Tutti. Barbie's* world was expanding, and covering all bases!

In 1968, the Mod reign was stronger than ever. A new word, "Psychedelic," was creeping up.

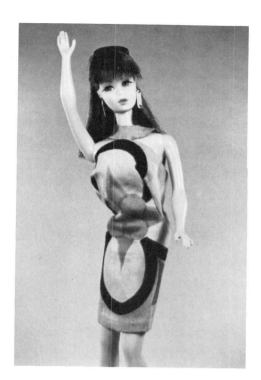

122. Short skirts, long straight hair and swingy earrings were the hallmark of fashion in this 1967 outfit, *Sunflower!*

123

124

Originally developed by the drug culture to describe a flashing light experience while on LSD, the word spilled over into teenage slang and meant "cool, and very modern." The top show of 1968 was "Rowan and Martin's Laugh-In." Hemlines were still creeping upwards and the boom children, now in college, were grooving to "Dance Concerts," a type of entertainment where you danced while a band played to a "mind blowing" light show.

Some teens, of course, would get caught up in the ever-blossoming "peace" ghettos of California and New York; some would die in the growing Vietnam war. Others would "alter consciousness" with the hallucinogenic

123. *Francie* had her own house and entertained *Black Francie!* Fashions are from left, 1971 *Zig-Zag Zoom* and 1966 *It's A Date.*

124. In 1971, Mattel had decided to offer another friend for *Francie* called *Becky*. The doll was made from the *Casey* head molds and was shown in catalogs. For some reason, the doll was never made. This box shows the logo for *Becky* that was sold for months. All this adds to the fun of *Barbie* collecting.

125. A 1969 and a 1968 *Talking Barbie* as they were originally sold. The 1968 doll in the case seems much more difficult to find.

126. A 1969 "Marlo Thomas" inspired *Barbie* models 1967 *Sparkle Squares*, while a 1967 *Twist 'N Turn Barbie* sports 1967s *Dancing Stripes*.

127. P.J. models *Check the Suit*, 1971, while *Stacey* with the 1969 short hair models 1970 *Lemon Kick*.

drugs available on any street corner. The largest group, thankfully, would just take the best from these trends and become "weekend" hippies, attending concerts dressed in wild clothing, then return back to the dorm to study for finals. Youth was asking to be wild and free. Many could not handle that much freedom!

1968 at Mattel saw the giant toy company dive headlong into the social issues of the day. *Barbie* got a black friend, *Christie*.

The statement this doll makes is really groundbreaking, for *Barbie* was crossing color lines to have a black best friend. *Christie* was a lovely girl who definitely was ethnically featured, but intelligent and pretty at the same time. In a country that just ten years before had separate drinking fountains for blacks and whites, this really was quite a step. The public found the connection wonderful, and blacks bought *Christie* as a companion for *Barbie*. It was a step in the right direction.

Also that year *Barbie* got a British friend, *Stacey*. Available as a platinum blonde or a dashing redhead, *Stacey* was Mod, but not quite as "far out" as *Twiggy*. Added to the dolls was a "talking" feature, similar to that used in the *Chatty Cathy* dolls of almost ten years earlier. The phrases uttered were typical teen sentences, performed by carefully selected actresses. The talking dolls would be around for a while, but proved troublesome as many broke easily. Today it is almost impossible to find one that still talks, even when sealed in the box.

Mention should be made that 1968 was the first year since 1961 that *Ken* was not available. The late 1960s were a hard time for teenage boys. An unfair war and even more unfair draft

128. Standard *Barbies*. Left is 1967, right is 1970. This doll was also offered as a mail-in offer for Campbell soup labels.

129. A 1969 *Talking P.J.* and *Talking Stacey*. The logo that year was "Everybody's Talking Barbie Talk." Even the fan club magazine was entitled *Barbie Talk*.

130. Throughout the Mod period, fashions reflected the British influence. Here 1969 dolls model Smasheroo and Snap-Dash!

system was forcing young men to either enlist, enroll in college (for the valued II-S deferment), or run away to Canada.

By eliminating Ken this very touchy year, Mattel avoided the obvious question of just what Ken's political beliefs were. Some news articles of the day picked up on this and one, in a mock interview with Barbie, asked her if he had run away to Canada. Always a lady, Barbie replied that yes, she missed him, but life goes on...

1969 saw another huge civil rights step for Mattel and Barbie. A television show called Julia debuted in 1968. By 1969, it was often rated number one of the week. Completely different, it featured the lovely Diahann Carroll as "Julia," a nurse raising a son while widowed. What made the show meaningful was that not only was Julia black, her husband had been killed in the line of duty in Vietnam. The show was not seen as a black show, but a show about an ordinary family that just happened to be black. Ironically, Diahann Carroll would say that the last leading black lady on a TV show was "Beulah," a 1950 sitcom about a maid!

The lovely Julia doll joined the Barbie line of licensed friends. This author groups family, friends, celebrity friends and acquaintances differently than others, but Julia was not billed as Barbie's friend on the packaging, only that she could also wear Barbie-sized fashions. This is, to me, the criteria for categorizing the Mattel dolls in Barbie's world.

Another great licensed friend for Barbie in 1969 was the Truly Scrumptious doll. Made with Francie's head and Barbie's body, she reflected the Victorian look of the movie she was based on, Chitty Chitty Bang Bang.

With some fanfare Ken returned. Completely redesigned, this new Ken was huskier and hunkier. Teenage standards had evolved from the quiet "boy next door" type, into a more athletic and stockier type of young man. This new Ken had a completely redesigned face with longish side-parted "Edwardian" hair and a new wardrobe. This was necessary because Ken could not fit in his old wardrobe. (Some authorities feel that this is the reason Ken was absent in 1968).

131. 1969 Twist 'N Turn dons 1969 Midi Magic! Hemlines were a real fashion statement in the late 1960s.

The Wonderful World of Barbie

MATTEL

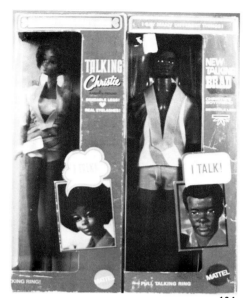

134

133. In 1969 and 1970, Mattel aimed dolls at Spanish speaking youth in this *Spanish Talking Barbie* and *Ken*. They were moderately successful, but the time was not right for ethnic dolls.

134. 1970 saw blacks start to search for their African roots. This *Talking Christie* and *Talking Brad* mirror that trend in ethnic outfits. The dolls were a success and tied *Barbie* into another culture.

135. A 1970 *Talking Barbie* models 1969 *Let's Have a Ball*, while a 1970 *Twist 'N Turn Barbie* models 1970 *Blue Royalty*.

136. A 1970 Diahann Carroll as *Julia* with her fashion, *Burr, Fur*. This doll was representative of the move to a blending of cultures.

135

132. A 1969-1970 store display. This smart merchandising allowed these displays to act as a permanant salesman, always on duty to show off the product. These are very rare and highly sought after today.

137. 1970 *Walking Jamie* with blonde and red hair. Sears often sold exclusive dolls and clothing. These are more valuable and harder to find than the regular line of dolls.

138. The *Barbie Twist 'N Turn* dolls. Left: 1968, 1969, 1970 and 1971 with centered eyes. These shrink-wrapped dolls created the term "never removed from box," to indicate that the shrink-wrapping was still intact.

139. A late 1960s *Barbie House*, very MODern in style, hosts *Stacy* in 1970 *Rare Pair*, 1970 *Walking Jaime* and *Talking Ken* in 1970 *Bold Gold*. Finishing the happy group are a 1970 *Twist 'N Turn Barbie* in 1969 *Glo-Go* and 1969 *Talking P.J.* wearing 1966 *Print Aplenty*.

Also new in 1969 was a "new" friend for *Barbie*. The *Midge* head mold had been brought back in the guise of *P.J.*, billed as just a friend of *Barbie*. With her "peace" beads wrapping her twin ponytails, and an orangy floral mini, she was the epitome of late 1960s chic.

By mid 1969, both *Barbie* and *Francie* would get hairstyle updates. *Barbie's* new look was a shoulder length "flip" style with ends curled up and a spit curl over her eye. *Francie* had basically the same style except for thicker bangs and a shorter "flip."

140. Among the many Sears exclusive gift sets are these two outfits. Many sets were available for *Barbie* and her friends over the years. Some outfits, such as this, look like Sears clothing.

141. Evening wear was still popular during the Mod period. Dress-up gowns such as *Silver Serenade* from 1971 and *Fab City* from 1969 were annual favorites.

142. After being absent in 1968, *Ken* returned newly designed in 1969, huskier and with an "Edwardian" hairstyle. Left is 1971 *V.I.P. Scene. Ken* models *Sea Scene*, 1971, and on right is 1970 *Big Business.*

143. 1970 *Living Barbie* was more posable than ever. Also issued the following year in a rare coin dot outfit, she had centered eyes, new for *Barbie*.

144. 1970 *Living Skipper* models *Wooly Winter* from the same year, while a 1970 *Living Barbie* dons 1971 *Super Scarf*. The mini skirt and "go go boots" were a popular look.

144

Both of these styles were based on the Marlo Thomas hairstyle from the television show "That Girl."

1970 saw the first disaster strike Mattel. The factory in Mexico, a primary manufacturing source since the Japanese factory was closed, was completely destroyed by a fire. The tragedy would signal the beginning of trouble for Mattel.

The dolls of 1970, however, were still of the highest quality. *Living Barbie* and *Living Skipper* were more posable than ever. A trade-in offer done the same way as the one in 1967 was arranged for *Skipper* dolls. For $1.99 a child could trade-in for new dolls.

Like before, the old dolls were donated to charity.

Christie, selling well, received her own boyfriend in *Brad*. Available in very "African" ethnic outfits, *Christie* and *Brad* symbolized the new black pride and awareness of African roots.

Sears, long a source of *Barbie* specials, made a friend for *Barbie*, *Walking Jamie*. Made from *Barbie* molds, her hair and coloring really made her seem different.

With the early 1970s came emphasis on hair care. *Francie* came with *Growin' Pretty Hair*, and as a *Hair Happenin's* doll with extra hairpieces. New for 1970 were more aquaintances

145. Late 1960s Sears *Talking Barbie* gift set. The artwork on these sets were a statement unto themselves. *Barbie's* outfit is trimmed in real mink!

146. *Barbie's Little Sister, Tutti* came in several play sets throughout the Mod period. Top is *Sundae Treat* and features *Todd,* her twin brother; left is *Walking My Dolly,* and right, *Night Night, Sleep Tight.*

147. The 1970s were very visible in this 1971 *Live Action Christie, Barbie* and *Ken.* Long straight center-parted hair and fringed psychedelic print outfits ushered in a new era.

for *Tutti. Nan 'N Fran,* a black doll and her doll; *Lori 'N Rori,* a blonde doll with a Teddy Bear; and *Angie 'N Tangie,* a brunette doll holding a blonde doll.

To satisfy Hispanic children, *Barbie* and *Ken* were available in 1970 as talking dolls that spoke Spanish! Often viewed today as "tokenism," these attempts to satisfy all children were actually quite advanced. Mattel was the only doll manufacturer that even acknowledged that America was made up of ALL ethnic backgrounds.

By 1971, the Mod movement had disintegrated, due mainly to the escalating Vietnam crisis. It seemed hard to party while high school friends were being drafted. The polarization

148

149

150

148. The *Malibu* dolls appeared in 1971. Featuring golden tans and long, straight blonde hair, they epitomized the "natural look" that was becoming popular in the early 1970s. 149. *Malibu Ken Surf's Up* gift set, a Sears exclusive, 1971. This set featured a very tan and blonde *Ken* that idealized the American dream of the "beach boy." 150. 1971 *Sun 'N Fun Buggy*. This great battery operated car was the only vehicle available for *Barbie* during this period. Seen are *Talking Barbie, Ken* and *Stacey.*

between those who thought we should be there an those who thought we should not even took its toll on fashion.

The "hippie," or someone who had great apathy, was becoming a national hero. Baby boom children were discovering that they could not control their own destiny as they once believed. This disenchantment led many to simply "drop out" of society. "Communes" were born, places where individuals who believed in shared love, peace and happiness could live together. Based on medieval principles of communal ownership, these places proved to be no utopia either as disease and drug use tainted the spoiled boom children.

During 1971, fashion adopted this "hippie" look, and suede fringe became the rage. Except for Italian movie stars who still sported false eyelashes and piled on curls, the "natural" look was "in." Long, straight hair, as seen on the children in the "Brady Bunch" on TV, was the newest look.

Live Action Barbie, Christie, P.J. and *Ken* were issued in 1971 in wild print clothing and heavy fringe. *Barbie, Christie* and *P.J.* had long, straight hair; *Ken* looked ready for Woodstock!

Some interesting new dolls appeared in 1971. A department store special *Barbie* with short, red hair and extra hairpieces was available, entitled *Barbie Hair Happenin's.* Also new were the *Malibu* dolls, available with gorgeous tans and California blonde straight hair a la Cheryl Tiegs, the top model of the day. An interesting *Francie* with an off-the-face flip style hairdo was also issued. *Skipper* got a new friend, *Fluff,* and both *Living Barbie* and *Living Skipper* were modified!

And the beat goes on...

151

152

151. The incoming "granny gown" craze can be seen in this 1972 *Barbie with Growin' Pretty Hair.* Contrasted next to her is the last of the Mod dolls, the 1971 version in a Mod-inspired dress. Times were changing!

152. One of the last of the TV families that exuded the "apple pie" Americanism was the "Brady Bunch." Starting in 1969, this show is important to *Barbie* collectors because Maureen McCormick, playing Marcia Brady and shown seated third from the left, was the child in several of the late 1960s *Barbie* commercials. Cindy Brady, (Susan Olsen) looked just like *Tutti, Barbie's Little Sister.*

VI. The Passive Seventies (1972-1976)

The registered trademarks, the trademarks and the copyrights appearing in italics within this chapter belong to Mattel, Inc., unless otherwise noted.

The early 1970s were uncertain years for the Handlers and Mattel. In January 1972, Mattel reported an unprecedented loss of 30 million dollars in revenue. By June the Handlers' lawyer, Seymour Rosenburg, would be gone, after selling off 80,000 shares of company stock for two million dollars.

In 1973, the Handlers were forced out of management and Art Spears, executive vice president in charge of operations, became president. The Securities Exchange Commission would later claim that during 1970-71, Mattel's managers had grossly violated standard accounting practices to gain much needed capital.

It was reported in an article in *Savvy, The Magazine for Executive Women*, May 1980, that this whole situation ended in 1978 with Ruth Handler and Seymour Rosenburg pleading no contest to ten counts of securities and mail fraud. She was fined, along with Rosenburg, to pay $57,000 and sentenced to serve 2500 hours of community service.

Time has made everyone evaluate just what did happen. In my opinion, the simple truth is that Mattel had growing pains. Hindsight points out that questionable advice coupled with adverse business conditions caused trouble to one of the most creative ladies in the doll world. It truly was the end of an era.

All of these problems, of course, affected the *Barbie* program. In 1972, for the first time, there were no fashion booklets packaged with the dolls. A simple move like this could save millions in production costs.

Actually, I feel that the dolls from 1972 and 1973 did not show the lack of quality the dolls and fashions from 1974-1976 would show. Changes may not have "caught up" yet because of a wealth of pre-designed dolls, clothes and accessories.

The year 1972 saw the introduction of *Walk Lively Ken, Barbie, Steffie* and *Miss America*. Laura Lee Shaefer, Miss America of 1972, was one of the most visible Miss Americas ever. She promoted her doll on Kellogg's Corn Flakes with a special mail-in offer, minus the walking stand that came with the dolls sold in stores.

153. A "Sweet 16" *Barbie* models her Bicentennial outfit!

Malibu P.J. was added to the *Malibu* line of dolls that year. Her head was made from the *Steffie* molds. That mold is used even in 1987 for *Barbie's* new friend, *Whitney!*

Teenagers were into activities, and the 1972 dolls had what would be called "busy" hands, or hands that opened and closed, allowing them to hold objects packaged with them like a

154. Although dated 1972 and available 1973 and 1974, this paper doll showed the earlier "talking" doll, obviously better quality for a photograph.

155. *Walk Lively Barbie and Ken, 1972.* These dolls are the epitome of early 1970s fashions. *Barbie's* long, straight, center-parted hair and bell-bottoms are typical period fashions, as are *Ken's* plaid pants!

TV set or a suitcase. The talking feature was still popular that year; all the "busy dolls" came in talking versions except *Francie*, mainly because her body was too small to hold the mechanism.

Available in "busy" form were *Barbie*, *Ken*, *Steffie* and *Francie*. Talking *Busy Dolls* were, *Barbie*, *Ken* and *Steffie*. The year 1972 saw the introduction of other "action" dolls, with *Pose 'N' Play Skipper* who had "swinging-free arms," and her tomboy friend, *Tiff*, a very rare doll today. *Tiff* was made from the *Fluff* molds and came dressed in jeans and a white tee shirt.

Barbie had to have some glamour so a new version of *Barbie* was added to the line, *Barbie with Growin' Pretty Hair*. It was interesting to note that "granny gowns," the official "hippie" dress-up clothing, was utilized for

Barbie. Also big that year was the "prairie look," evident in both *Barbie* and *Francie* outfits. American fashion

157

---

157. 1973 was the year of women's rights. *Barbie* made a wonderful statement by becoming a doctor! In the early 1960s, she was allowed only to be a nurse.

158. A very rare *Put ons and Pets* outfit from 1972. This wonderful period outfit featured "hot pants," the latest youth craze. *Barbie's* dog is a great addition to this ensemble!

158

---

156. "The Partridge Family," starring Shirley Jones, David Cassidy and Susan Dey, exemplified the typical "flower power" family of the early 1970s. *Movie Star News* photograph.

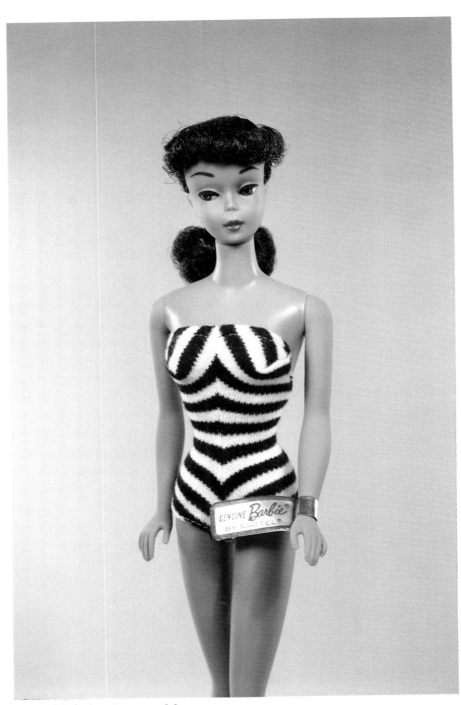

159. 100th Anniversary Montgomery Wards' *Barbie*. This was supposed to be the "original" *Barbie* (a very misused term), but actually was an exact reproduction of a number five doll.

was really at a low point as far as glamour was concerned.

1972 was a boring year for American pop culture. Vietnam was a despised venture; "causes" were dying rapidly as teens realized that the government had misled them about the major issues of the day. "Apathy" was the password of the early 1970s.

The only highpoint of the year was that an old established firm, Montgomery Ward, was celebrating its 100th anniversary. Long a source of gift sets and other specials for *Barbie*. Wards had Mattel reissue the "original" *Barbie* doll for its anniversary celebration. Made to look like the number five ponytail, this doll is much sought after today by ardent collectors. Even Mattel thought of this doll as the "original" doll, for she really was one of the first of the heavily mass-marketed dolls. This thinking even went unchanged in 1984, for Mattel publicity shots showed a number five *Barbie*, in 8in (20cm) by 10in (25cm) glossies as the "original" *Barbie*. This has added much to the confusion with the general public about the value of the early dolls.

1973 saw an American obsession with hair. It was a natural thing. Those in established jobs could not wear the long, straight hairdos associated with

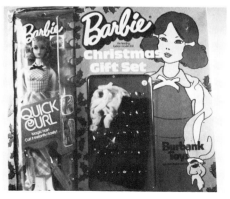

160. *Talking Busy Barbie*. These dolls were interesting in that they had a "serf," or peasant haircut, "hot pants," and the "busy" hands that could open and close.

161. In 1973, *Barbie* got a new friend, *Quick Curl Kelley*. *Francie* was on her way out, but made a last try as a brunette.

162. *Quick Curl Barbie* was so popular, she was issued in the gift set distributed by Burbank Toys in the United Kingdom. An extra outfit was included.

the "flower children." Men in "corporate" jobs, thought by many to be part of the "establishment" and over 30, could not have the long "shag" haircut made famous by David Cassidy on "The Partridge Family." In fact, the *Barbie* and *Ken* of this era could well be the Keith and Laurie Partridge (Laurie played by Susan Dey) from this show. Laurie, with her long, straight hair and Keith, with his flowered shirts and shag cut, were the perfect uninvolved teen couple.

Mattel responded to this trend by issuing *Mod Hair Ken*. The musicals, "Godspell" and "Jesus Christ, Superstar" of 1973 gave young Americans historical and biblical reasons why long stringy hair was okay.

"Quick Curl Hair," the big feature on all the dolls that year, could go from straight and flat, to fluffy and curly with a twist of a wand. The secret was a wire fiber rooted into the hair. The lead dolls were *Quick Curl Barbie*, *Skipper*, *Francie* (as a rare brunette) and *Miss America*. *Barbie* got a new *Quick Curl* friend in *Kelley*, a lovely redhead made form the *Steffie* molds. *Malibu Christie*, a black doll, joined the *Sun Set* that year.

The company troubles were evident in 1973, for leftover stock was issued in "baggies," (plastic bags with cardboard tops), containing old dolls.

1974 was an interesting year in *Barbie* doll history. This was *Barbie's* 16th birthday. Actually, if you count backwards, only 15 years had passed since *Barbie* was introduced at Toy Fair in 1959. Eager to recapture lost revenues, the new leadership at Mattel

163. The "busy" series of 1972-73 found another new friend for *Barbie* in *Busy Steffie.* **164.** Early 1970s *Barbie* fashions reflected the looks of the day with longer skirts, the ever popular miniskirt and, of course, formal wear. **165.** Charlotte Johnson, the designer of all the *Barbie* fashions the entire time the Handlers were at Mattel, came the closest yet in the early 1970s to a name credit. The packaging of some deluxe outfits featured a mention of "C.J." who traveled "world wide" to find fabrics for *Barbie* fashions.

used the patent date, 1958, as the official date of *Barbie's* birth. Because *Barbie* was around 16 years old, the tie-in was a natural.

Unfortunately, quality was not the goal of Mattel in 1974, profit was. In order to stay afloat, it was necessary to design catchy, glittery products that did not cost much to produce. The *Sweet 16 Barbie* lacked even the essentials of earlier dolls. Gone were the rich eyelashes, rooted in the plastic, and the hand done hairstyles. In their place was cheaper vinyl with poorly painted features and a "shag" cut that unfortunately, was the "in" style.

In all fairness, the *Sweet 16 Barbie*, when one looks backwards, is a lovely doll that looks 16! Earlier dolls had become so "couture" that *Barbie* could have easily been 35 under all that makeup! This doll capitalized on the fresh face look of current cover girls like Cheryl Tiegs, whose "clean make-up" face glowed from Sears catalogs. In a last ditch effort to trim costs further, wrist tags were discontinued, a move which again saved several million dollars a year for Mattel. Besides, the current customer of *Barbie*, younger and less sophisticated than teens of the early 1960s, did not care about such amenities.

New in 1974 was the *Sports Set*. These dolls included *Sun Valley Barbie*, a ski queen with a golden tan like Suszi Chaffee; *Sun Valley Ken*, her male counterpart; *Newport Barbie*, dressed

166. In 1974, a year early, *Barbie* turned "Sweet 16." A special promotional doll with extra outfits consisting of "cut offs" and a "tank top" was issued. This set was bought in Canada and features both French and English on the packaging. 167. 1974 *Sports Set* dolls. *Sun Valley Barbie* and *Newport Barbie*, made from the *Malibu* dolls. 168. In 1974, Sears had a *Barbie Baby Sits* exclusive, using the baby from Mattel's *Sunshine Family*. This was the first issue of such a set since 1965. The set could give girls a chance to play "mommy" with *Barbie*, a role which never suited the doll!

169. The 1975 Olympic Games resulted in a 2 million dollar promotional tie-in with Mattel. *Barbie* wore the gold medal of many countries including Canada, with its Maple Leaf. The set, center, is a Sears exclusive. The paper doll shows *Cara* and *Curtis, Barbie's* black friends.

170. 1975 *Free Moving Cara* and *Barbie*. The quality reflects a company in crisis.

for sailing; and *Yellowstone Kelley*, ready for camping.

Of note in 1974 was the issue of *Busy Steffie* stock in a plastic bag, titled, *Babs*. (Babs had been the name of earlier *Barbie* competitors.)

Still eager to capture the collector, Montgomery Wards issued a *Mod Hair Ken* dressed in an exclusive tuxedo, of the "tacky" variety one would wear to "show off" in the mid 1970s!

Americans were bored out of their minds in 1975. After five years of doing nothing, they were ready to celebrate. The 1975 Olympic Games gave them just such a chance. Never in the history of the Olympics had there been such a fanfare! Mattel tied into the campaign with a 2 million dollar advertising budget! *Gold Medal Barbie*, complete with her award medal, appeared in the stores as early as January 1975. Usually Mattel launched new dolls in the late Spring.

The doll was a regular *Malibu* doll, (every athlete has a tan, of course!), dressed in a one-piece red, white and blue swimsuit. Mail-in coupons allowed the child to send for a record book to keep track of the events and an iron-on shield for shirt or jacket.

A few weeks later other *Gold Medal* dolls reached the market, and included a *Barbie Skier*, *Barbie Skater*, *Ken Skier* and a *P.J. Gymnast*. Separate Olympic outfits were available for the almost defunct *Francie*, and *Skipper* as well. Sears had exclusive dolls with extra clothes for post Olympic events. Whitman issued a special sports theme paper doll book.

These dolls are especially noteworthy because they mirrored Mattel's new management philosophy that *Barbie* SHOULD have an identity that girls can relate to. Children of this period were far less imaginative than

171. The *Now Look Ken*. Did we REALLY look like that? It is hard to believe that is *Ken* beneath that hair! Dolls like this tell the story of American pop culture so very well!

172. *Malibu Ken*, *Barbie* and *P.J.* on their way to a peace march! Dolls dressed like this bring back memories to the baby boom children who did it all.

173. A rare *Growing-Up Skipper* fashion. This controversial doll grew breasts when her arm was turned!

174. The incredibly poor quality of this *Barbie plus 3* set available in 1975 is proof that Mattel was having problems. The doll is a nightmarish imitation of *Barbie*, and the clothing is "goodwill box" quality!

their predecessors and needed a visual, active role model. The new *Gold Medal Barbie*, made from the smiling *Stacey* molds, had a confident, secure personality that post Vietnam children needed. Many of these children were not getting that security at home the way the "Leave It to Beaver" generation had. Today's mother was "burned out," either from the drug culture or peace causes. *Barbie* was offereing these children a fresh start at life, untainted by years they did not help shape or understand.

Also introduced in 1975 were *Free Moving Barbie, Ken, P.J.* and the black *Cara* and *Curtis* dolls. The need for *Barbie* to be blonde and white was still there, but her friends could be black. It would be another five years before *Barbie* could be seen as belonging to other cultures.

The big controversy of the year was a doll called *Growing Up Skipper*. With a twist of her arm, her budding breasts sprouted, and she grew 3/4th of an inch (2cm)! Every newspaper in the country carried stories about the "immorality" of the doll, but in reality, children loved her. She was a huge success to children who saw the natural development of *Skipper* as healthy.

Also added to the *Quick Curl* line for 1975 was *Quick Curl Cara*, a black doll. Department stores got a lovely new doll, *Hawaiian Barbie*, made from the heavily used *Steffie* molds.

1975 was the beginning of a turning point in Mattel profits after the lean years of the early 1970s. Revenues were coming in sufficiently to launch an exciting new line for 1977!

1976 started off with a new logo for *Barbie*. Most collectors, myself included, do not think the new logo tells the fashion image of *Barbie* as well as the old, script logo.

For 1976, the *Quick Curl* dolls were issued in deluxe sets with "falls,"

or hairpieces that could be attached to create glamorous new play possibilities. Long hair for men was still in style (although would go out with a "snip" next year), and Mattel issued *Now Look Ken* with super long rooted hair.

For those traditionally minded, *Ballerina Barbie* was available. Dressed in a typical ballet costume, her black friend, *Cara*, also was ready for practice.

Growing Up Skipper got a new friend, *Growing Up Ginger*, basically the same doll with dark hair; *Barbie* and *Skipper* both got Bicentennial outfits featuring colonial patriots marching for freedom.

The passive seventies were, thankfully, drawing to a close! Just ahead was the razzle dazzle of a new beat.

175. Even the Whitman paper dolls of the period such as this one showed the lack of quality apparent in *Barbie* products. The clothing illustrated is contrived, and not even Mattel fashions. By 1977, quality would return!

VII. Disco Daze (1977-1979)

By the late 1970s, the baby boomers were restless. Having spent the last ten years involved in peace marches, sit-ins and demonstrations, they were weary of "causes." Haight-Ashbury, the California haven for "hippies" and "flower children" was overrun with disease, crime and poverty. Suddenly the "establishment" did not look so bad after all.

Little by little, women began to dress up. Gradually at first, because it was not easy to surrender those jeans and army-navy store jackets, but slowly glamour began to return.

In New York, nightclubs were opening up that were devoted to playing the elaborate music of late 1970s. That music was "DISCO!" Originally played in Latin clubs as a throwback to calypso, the music spread to the black clubs, the gay clubs, and then to all America. Soon "chic" places such as "Studio 54" opened in New York, and almost overnight it was fashionable to dress up and go out! The late 1970s, like the Roaring Twenties, came right after a war, Vietnam, and people were ready to let the corks pop. They were tired of Richard Nixon, acid rock and long dragging bell-bottoms. Suddenly people wanted to look plastic! Bianca Jagger and Calvin Klein became the new "celebs" to watch; a lovely baby boomer named Farrah Fawcett-Majors

was the star of a TV show called, "Charlie's Angels." The impact that Farrah had on our culture was similar to that of Marilyn Monroe in the 1950s.

Her dazzling wide smile and sun-streaked hair were the epitome of late 1970s' glamour. Suddenly Bloomingdales became the "in" spot to shop. Times were changing very quickly.

Mattel spotted this trend and responded. By 1977, most of their economic problems left over from the previous years were under control. *Barbie* could once again be a fashion leader and representative of today's young women.

With much fanfare, Mattel announced the arrival of *Superstar Barbie!* The resemblance to Farrah was amazing. Not only that, but her arms bent in a glamourous pose and she wore jewelry, absent from the dolls during the product safety code years. Her dress was long and swingy and she sported a sparkly boa! With her came *Superstar Fashions* that were miles away from the outfits one would have worn only a handful of years before!

176. This *Promotional Superstar Barbie*, with face modeled after Farrah Fawcett-Majors, launched a new era for *Barbie* in 1977.

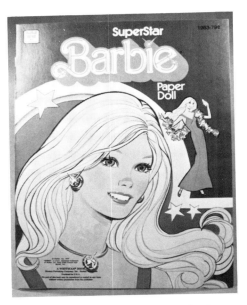

177. *Barbie's* glamorous new look was captured in this paper doll from Whitman, 1977.

178. Special outfits for *Superstar Barbie* were issued in 1977 that signaled the return of real quality to Mattel. On the left is *Romantic White*, right is *Silver Shimmer*.

Adding to the glamour was a *Star 'Vette* that allowed *Barbie* to arrive at the disco in style. Not mentioned in the company catalogs was a *Promotional Superstar Barbie* that had a slinky, glittery dress and white rabbit stole. Afraid to push the new look too far, the 1977 catalog is mainly made up of carryovers from other years. Also, Mattel was just getting back on its feet.

In 1978, the disco scene was in full swing. Every major city had dance clubs that were like speakeasies. One pulled up in a fancy car and made a grand entrance. Dance contests were every place, with prizes that ranged from dinner for two at a local "hot spot" to a trip around the world.

For teenage boys, this spelled trouble. Suddenly the best dancer in the class had all the dates, and not the best football player. Clothing long labeled as "sisified" was in style, and "in" boys spent hours at the hairstylist (barbershop was an old man's term!) getting the latest razor cut. The style-conscious male was getting all the attention. The jock was out.

To meet this trend, Mattel issued, in 1978, *Superstar Ken*. Dressed in a navy blue polyester jumpsuit with flare pants, he also sported "shades" (sunglasses to the unknowing) and much jewelry. A deluxe set was issued with both dolls in the box that looks like it was dropped out of Studio 54 in

179. The back of the *Superstar Barbie Fashions'* boxes had spectacular artwork that told the story of *Barbie's* disco nights.

180. By 1978, the *Superstar Barbie Fashions* were even more glamorous as disco swept America. Better ideas and fabrics were used this year, but the outfits simply had a stock number and were not named in the catalog.

New York! *Superstar Christie, Barbie's* black friend joined the party.

Another lead doll that year was *Fashion Photo Barbie*, which utilized the superstar molds and took *Barbie* back into the world of modeling. Her picture could be taken while she twirled a la Loretta Young in a chiffon gown.

Joining the *Barbie* family of friends in 1977-1978 were the Osmonds, *Donny, Marie* and *Jimmy*. The "Donny and Marie" show was also taking Americans back to glamour, yet discreetly, every Friday evening as Marie announced that she was "just a little bit country," while Donny was "just a little bit rock and roll." The dolls were lovely and cleverly made with definite resemblances to the stars. Gone, however, was the "friend" tie-in to *Barbie*,

as they were just the same size, yet, in my opinion, not part of the *Barbie* family. Added to this in the 1978 Mattel catalog were *Kitty O'Neil*, a deaf race car driver, *Kate Jackson*, "Sabrina" on "Charlie's Angels" and *Cheryl Ladd*, who replaced Farrah in that same show as Jill Monroe's sister, Chris. Again, I do not consider these dolls part of the *Barbie* family because no mention was made in the campaign or on the boxes about them being friends of *Barbie*, only that the same clothing would fit them.

1978 saw many "specials" that the collector should try to add to his/her collection. A *Malibu Barbie Fashion Combo*, sold in the Philadelphia area only at Best Products, was a gift set featuring a *Malibu Barbie* and extra clothes. Another great set was *Beautiful Bride Barbie*, available only in department stores and featured the new superstar molds.

Even True Value Hardware stores had a *Superstar Barbie Fashion Change-Abouts* set that was only available the month before Christmas, 1978, and featured a doll with a mix-and-match wardrobe. A set called *Superstar Barbie in the Spotlight* appeared as a department store special and was available in two versions.

In 1977 and 1978 an 18in (46cm) *Supersize Barbie* appeared in the stores, along with the black version, *Supersize Christie*. It failed to attract attention, despite the introduction of a department store special, *Supersize Bridal Barbie*, because even though the doll was incredibly well made, the public just did not think of *Barbie* as that size. Tried as an experiment because another fashion doll, *Candy*, had been doing well in both sizes, Mattel realized with mixed emotions that *Barbie* was petite and not that tall. These dolls, the failures as it were, will be valuable to future collectors because of their short shelf life.

By 1979, things were slowing down a bit. Romance had begun to combine with glamour. Mattel issued *Kissing Barbie*, a doll that could pucker her lips and plant a kiss on *Ken*. The doll was frilly and feminine, and not very popular. A department store special with an extra gown was issued but it,

181. The face of the late 1970s, Farrah Fawcett-Majors. Her glowing tan and toothy grin, along with her signature hairstyle, would launch a new doll and a new era for *Barbie*. American girls would copy her look for the next ten years! *Movie Star News* photograph.

182. The movie *Saturday Night Fever* (Paramount, 1977), would propel dancing and dressing to new heights. The classic film portrayed a young dancer (John Travolta) using his talents for escape to a better life. The fashions and crazes it would create lasted for years! *Movie Star News* photograph.

183. By 1978, *Superstar Barbie* was joined with *Superstar Ken,* in this gift set, available only in selected stores. *Superstar Ken* took the concept of *Barbie's* boyfriend away from all-American and into the realm of sophisticated nightlife.

184. *Superstar Ken and Barbie* exemplified the return of dressing up and going out in America. They were the epitome of the "beautiful people."

185. Many licensed products helped familiarize the new face of *Barbie* to the public. Ambassador Greetings, a division of Hallmark, issued two greeting cards with the new doll, and Golden Books published a *Barbie* fantasy featuring the new *Superstar Barbie*.

186. Special gift sets were available in 1978 for *Superstar Barbie* such as this set on the left for department stores called *Superstar Barbie in the Spotlight* and the set on the right, *Superstar Barbie Fashion Change-abouts* available at True Value Hardware.

too, failed to meet expectations.

Ballerina Barbie, however, was made for the girl with other dreams, and added to the department store special called *Ballerina Barbie on Tour*, which featured the costumes from "The Nutcracker." Even Sears had an exclusive outfit with a record for the doll.

The lead doll of the year was a tame *Pretty Changes Barbie*, interesting only in that her hair was short, which was rare. With her came a blonde "fall" and a brunette wig. The quality was just not there, and her popularity was not that of the *Superstar Barbie* dolls. Clearly Americans wanted the type of woman who was exciting and glamorous.

Barbie's Little Sister, Skipper, became a teenager this year, with a new, grown-up image that, too, would prove unpopular. Notice also that the 1977-1979 lines were basically small compared to other years that would follow. Mattel was still, as was the nation, floundering to find itself.

Many young Americans will always remember the period from 1977-1979 as a fast moving time of dancing, glamour, bright lights and excitement. The problem was that change was so overdue, that it was happening too rapidly! Mattel, afraid to take too many chances after the "fall" of a few years before, was playing safe with a smaller line that covered all bases. Glamour queen, disco star, fashion

---

187. Something had to pay for all the glamourous nights at the disco, and in 1978, *Barbie* resumed her career as a fashion model with *Fashion Photo Barbie*. 188. The *Malibu* dolls had been best sellers for years. This set, *Malibu Barbie Fashion Combo*, was sold in Philadelphia only at Best Products. The collector should always be watching for specials such as this, as they are rapidly discontinued.

model, romantic heroine, all were adjectives to describe the *Barbie* doll of the late 1970s. Just ahead were the energetic 1980s, and a bit slower pace!

189. In 1977-1978, *Donny* and *Marie Osmond* were available. Some call them part of the *Barbie* family, but the only tie-in was that they were the same size as *Barbie* and *Ken*. Mattel themselves did not want a connection to these dolls as being "friends" of *Barbie*, and placed the dolls in the rear of the Mattel catalogs. They are, however, interesting historical additions to a *Barbie* collection.

190. The disco period had to have some tradition for *Barbie*. She was issued as a department store special bride in these two dolls, available in 1976-77 on the left, with real rooted eyelashes, and the "old" *Barbie* face. Also marketed in 1978 was the new *Superstar Barbie* dressed as a bride. Both were called *Beautiful Bride Barbie*.

191. The success of a competing fashion doll that was issued in two sizes hastened Mattel to issue *Barbie* in this 18in (46cm) size. As a department store special bride in 1978, she still did not capture the market intended. The petite image of *Barbie* was impossible to break.

191

192. By 1979, quality was being seen everywhere in Mattel products. This matching outfit set for *Barbie* and *Ken* called *City Sophisticate* came in solid cardboard boxes with clothing labels and the old trappings of quality that made Mattel famous in the 1960s.

193. Despite the glamour emphasis, ballerinas and brides were still popular with little girls, especially those under five. *Ballerina Barbie on Tour* was a popular 1979 department store special that featured the doll and costumes from "The Nutcracker."

194. Romance entered into the disco scene with the new found popularity of the romance novel. *Kissing Barbie* on the left was issued for mass-market stores (this doll has the rare banged hair-do), and on the right as a department store special with extra gown.

195. Unusual because of her short, blonde hair, this *Pretty Changes Barbie* of 1979 helped teach a young girl about hairstyles. Her popularity was not as great as anticipated because little girls pictured *Barbie* with long blonde hair.

VIII.
The Energetic
Eighties
(1980-1987)

By 1980, America's love affair with disco was winding down. Many reasons can be cited for this, most notable being that so many people wanted to enter the "big" name clubs in major cities, that the doormen of these establishments were picking and choosing who could grace the dance floor. Americans were simply not used to being denied access to someplace they were willing to pay exorbitant sums of money to enter. These high prices were another deterrent to the continuation of the club culture started in the late 1970s.

Tired of wearing jeans since Vietnam, American women were not ready to stop dressing up. Even men were wearing colors once deemed "unmasculine" and the dolls reflect these trends.

Mattel in 1980 released *Beauty Secrets Barbie*, billed as having the longest hair ever on a *Barbie* doll. Her main feature was that her wrists were jointed so that she could hold a brush. A panel on her back made her arms move realistically. Along with her was a black version, named *Beauty Secrets Christie*, which was basically the same doll.

Men were starting to get into shape. Of course, all that disco dancing had

196. The 1980s show *Barbie* a proud, black woman astronaut, setting an example for everyone that "We girls CAN do anything...right, *Barbie?*"

197. The roller disco craze allowed American families to dance together on skates! *Roller Skating Barbie* and *Ken* from 1980 strut their stuff!

198. A rare *Beauty Secrets Barbie* store display. One hundred of these special plastic bubble displays were sent at random to Mattel accounts. This display was found in Hartford, Connecticut. Grooming and glamour were obsessions with American teens.

199. *Barbie* doll collectors have formed groups which meet annually to swap dolls and ideas. These convention souvenirs show a 1980 *Beauty Secrets Barbie* wearing a banner that says "21 Years of *Barbie*." The doll on the right is a specially dressed 1984 *Loving You Barbie* for *Barbie's* 25th birthday in New York. The center doll is a *Sun Gold Malibu Barbie*, dressed for the 1986 Phoenix, Arizona, convention.

already started to chip away at the flab, and men seemed eager to join the burgeoning health movement. A new *Sport and Shave Ken*, was out that year. Billed as "all man," (a phrase that would die out with the word "macho"), his main feature was a magic marker beard that could be "shaved off" with water, His extra "dress" outfit was a pair of sweat pants, sneakers and polo shirt. The advertising even dared to show a little boy joining in the fun of playing with this doll, but *Ken* was still sold in the "doll aisle," making him still taboo for most boys.

Available were *Black Barbie* and *Hispanic Barbie*. Mattel still felt the need to have their unquestionable ethnic backgrounds on the boxes.

Two of the most interesting new dolls for 1980 were *Super Teen Skipper* and her boyfriend, *Scott*. Could it be possible that *Barbie's Little Sister*, *Skipper*, had actually grown up? As previously mentioned, the big controversy over *Grownin' Up Skipper* had sent her back to childhood. Suddenly the psychologists at Mattel felt that the timing was right for another try at "teendom" for *Skipper*. Little girls were more eager than ever to grow up. Many fourth graders knew more about hair and makeup than their mothers did. Perhaps a teenage *Skipper* would work.

Accompanied by a skateboard, *Skipper* also had a ball gown! Her boyfriend, *Scott*, looked very much like "Bobby" on *"The Brady Bunch,"* (played by Michael Lookingland). In order to succeed, *Scott* had to be "hunky" enough to attract *Skipper*, but not overly sexy to offend anyone. In my opinion, he WAS too sexy. Children who had identified with *Skipper* being younger did not want to see the threat of a boyfriend in her life just yet. *Scott* was rapidly discontinued, and *Skipper* was eased back into the role of hoping she would "grow up" just like *Barbie*.

By late 1980, Americans had found a way to incorporate disco into their lives again, this time as a family! The new hero of the day was, of all places, the local roller skating rink! Now everyone in the family could spin, twirl and gyrate together on skates. This truly united disco music, exercise and the family as never before.

The movie industry responded to this "fad" by issuing catchy movies about roller skating that ranged from great to awful. Memorable was *Roller Boogie* with Linda Blair (remember her years earlier as Reagan in *The Exorcist?*) spinning more than just her head! *Skatetown U.S.A.* rapidly followed.

Mattel rapidly responded to this by issuing later in the year a beautiful set of dolls, *Roller Skating Barbie* and *Roller Skating Ken*. Dressed in matching, well-designed outfits, their skates were very lifelike. Unfortunately, America was moving at a rapid pace, on the rink and off, and the dolls were not around long.

Interestingly, 1980 was the 21st birthday of the *Barbie* doll. The occasion was completely ignored officially by Mattel, who was worried about taking *Barbie* out of the realm of a teenager. The media, however, played up this event with much publicity. Soon, however, with the arrival of "Dynasty" on ABC television, older women would be glamorized.

In 1980, the average little girl thought *Barbie* was 16-21. By 1987, some girls pictured her as old as 40! This was easy to do when Jaclyn Smith and Farrah Fawcett approached this age. *Barbie's* 25th birthday would not be ignored.

1981 saw glamour more popular

Introducing My First Barbie: The new Barbie doll designed for younger girls.

200. Mattel, eager to expand its market to the younger child, issued My First Barbie in 1981. This ad, from *Family Circle*, shows actress Heather O'Rourke with her doll.

201. Mattel wanted to encourage the collecting of *Barbie* dolls by adults, and acquired a list of collectors. These people were sent company catalogs annually, as well as a Christmas card, such as this one from 1981. As the number of collectors grew from hundreds to thousands, this practice had to be discontinued!

202. As disco music died down, country music revved up! In 1981, *Western Ken* and *Barbie*, and horses *Midnight* and *Dallas* appeared. *Barbie* could "wink" a hello and carried an autographed album cover. Her hairdo is a copy of Farrah Fawcett's style in "Charlie's Angels," a popular TV show.

203. Blacks had always viewed *Barbie* as white. In 1980, a *Black Barbie* was introduced. By 1982, *Magic Curl Barbie* was black, making no mention of such on the packaging, thus giving *Barbie* many identities for children of all races. Naturally *Barbie* needed *Ken*, so he, too, was issued in a black version.

than ever. Nighttime soaps such as "Dallas" and "Dynasty" were making "costume" dressing an art. Matching coats and hats to dresses were making a comeback that had not been seen since Joan Crawford in *Mildred Pierce* in 1945. Nolan Miller, the designer on the "Dynasty" set envisioned himself much like Adrian, THE designer of the 1930s, and wanted American women to look like movie stars. Mattel issued *Golden Dream Barbie* with the "Quick Curl" hair feature used once before and gave her a *Dream'Vette* to ride in.

Some Americans were finding a new thrill in country music, as a

204. Mattel created "specials" for department stores and specialty shops over the years. Usually including the lead doll for the year, something extra was added such as an additional outfit or item for the child. These sets rapidly disappear from store shelves and increase in value to the collector. From left, 1980 *Beauty Secrets Barbie Pretty Reflections*, 1981 *Golden Dream Barbie Golden Nights*, 1982 *Pink and Pretty Barbie* and 1983 *Twirley Curls Barbie*. 205. Additional department store special sets. 1984 *Loving You Barbie*, 1985 *Happy Birthday Barbie* and 1986 *Tropical Barbie Deluxe Gift Set*. 206. *Pink and Pretty Barbie* from 1982 sits at her *Electronic Piano*, a fabulous accessory that actually played! The framed picture was available by mail from Mattel.

207. 1983 *Barbie & Friends Gift Set*. In this rare set of three dolls in the same box, *Barbie* was dressed like a "Valley Girl" and *P.J.* was explained to be her cousin.

208. 1983 *Barbie & Ken Campin' Out Set*. Not since 1977 did *Barbie* and *Ken* come packaged together. These sets were not mass marketed and were available only in the western half of the United States.

statement away from the materialism of the "Dynasty" type of lifestyle. Singers such as Dolly Parton were crossing the line. Since many disco singers were one hit only stars, she and others like her were gaining in popularity. Country music was crossing over on the pop charts and getting away from its "hick" image.

The timing was right for *Western Barbie* and friends! An unusual doll, this *Barbie* could "wink" at the audience, and came with "album cover" pictures for her to autograph. Her hair was so VERY much a Farrah copy that it underwent three changes in one year. Her horse, *Dallas*, was issued, along with *Western Ken* and *Skipper*.

New for 1981 was the *My First Barbie*. In a brilliant ad campaign, Mattel showed a very young child (Heather O'Rourke of later *Poltergeist* fame!) playing safely with a *Barbie* doll that had smooth legs and special clothes. The thinking was to capture the younger market and keep it until the child "grew up," something which was happening by fourth grade. As more and more publicity arrived about the "collectibility" of the older *Barbie* dolls, little girls began to play with *Barbie* longer; having many older dolls gave one a kind of "status" with school chums. Fortunately for Mattel, today older girls are still displaying some of the more collectible dolls in their rooms as "shelf dolls," thus giving doll collecting respectability.

The 1980s saw a major breakthrough for civil rights. Up until these years, the public had viewed *Barbie* as white. As mentioned previously, a black *Francie* doll had been rebuffed by blacks themselves in the late 1960s. *Christie*, *Barbie's* black friend had been a success in her own right. Issued as a "companion" doll to *Barbie*, it was

209. 1984 was the 25th birthday of the *Barbie* doll! Mattel launched a major publicity campaign, such as this ad from *Playthings Magazine*, February 1984, proclaiming that an American legend had turned 25!

obvious that black children would play more with *Christie* as in examples such as *Superstar Christie.*

Finally, a breakthrough came in 1980 when *Black Barbie* was introduced. With a phrase borrowed from the TV show "Good Times." *Black Barbie* was "dynamite." Blacks were joyous to receive *Black Barbie* into their households, as they were no longer trying to be white to succeed in a white dominated society, but were accepting being black as something to be proud of.

The real breakthrough came with *Magic Curl Barbie*, an historic moment, for gone was the word "black" on the box. Both the white and black versions of this doll were identically dressed and packaged! For the first time in 23 years, *Barbie* was available as either black or white, without finding a "place" for the black version. This

trend continues today. ALL the lead dolls every year have a black and white issue. This is a great step for blacks in the US, and *Barbie* helped do it!

The disco craze was not fully dead, nor by any means was the health kick. Mattel issued *Fashion Jeans Barbie* and *Fashion Jeans Ken* in pink shirts and designer jeans complete with *Barbie's* own signature on the back pocket a la Calvin Klein and Gloria Vanderbilt. The newest upscale way to still wear blue jeans was to wear designer ones! *All Star Ken*, who not as macho as *Sport and Shave Ken*, lifted weights and had a flexible arm muscle.

The *International Barbies*, started in 1981 for collectors, added Eskimo and India to their growing numbers. These dolls are wonderfully made and destined to be quite valuable in the future. By 1987, there would be 14 in the series.

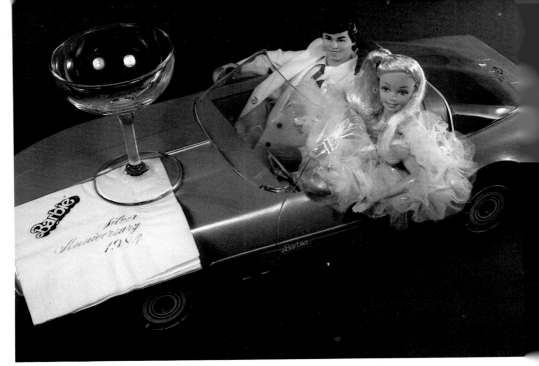

210. A special party was held for *Barbie* on Valentine's Day, 1984, in New York City, by invitation only. Souvenirs included a champagne glass and napkins printed for the occasion. *Crystal Barbie* and *Ken* enjoyed the ride in their *Silver Vette*.

211. *Loving You Barbie*, *Black Ken* and *Sweet Roses P.J.* attend the 25th celebration in the *Dream Carriage*, made just for the European market and one of the loveliest accessories ever made!

1983 was really a quiet year in our culture. There were lots of choices. *Angel Face Barbie*, who looked like sweetness and light, had cosmetics tied into Chesebrough-Ponds, Inc., and *Horse Lovin's Barbie, Ken and Skipper* kept the country idea alive with "red leather" jeans and "sheepskin" vests. *Skipper* got her own horse, *Honey*.

Hair was still popular, so another long hair doll appeared, *Twirly Curls Barbie*. Her beautiful long blonde hair could be styled with the help of a machine that twisted strands together. Another racial breakthrough came this year with an Hispanic version of *Twirly Curls Barbie*. The box showed an obviously Hispanic child playing with the doll; the entire box was in English-Spanish. No mention of her being Hispanic was on the box, again allowing *Barbie* to just be *Barbie* and not labeled. Available also was a black version. Now *Barbie* could truly be seen, like Santa Claus, as being whatever race a child wanted her to be. It was Ruth Handler's concept of a child projecting her identity on the doll at its best.

Dressing up was still important and *Dream Date Barbie* and *Ken* proved that with gorgeous satin-looking gowns and tuxedos. Most interesting was the issue of *Dream Date P.J.* in the same gown, but in another color. *Barbie* needed a friend to wear her clothes, but *Christie* was no longer used in this manner. The relationship of *P.J.* to *Barbie* had still yet to be explained.

Collectors eagerly awaited the arrival of two new friends for *Barbie* this year, *Tracy* and *Todd*, who were getting married. Most collectors were disappointed that *Tracy*, who used the P.J. face molds beautifully, had a sickly cast to her and washed out makeup as she was solely manufactured in the Phillipine factory. Even more disappointing was *Todd*, who was just *Ken*

212. 1985 saw more women in the work force than ever before. *Day to Night Barbie* was an important woman executive, complete with attaché case and credit cards. Of course, in the evening, her look converted to glamour by reversing her outfit. Next to her is the rare Hispanic version sold in select areas. This was again a positive racial image enhancer. 213. The aerobic trend to fitness was shown by *Great Shape Barbie, Ken* and *Skipper*. Photograph courtesy Mattel, Inc.

with different eye color. It was a shame an interesting concept could not have been more developed.

Finally in 1983, a gift set appeared that contained *Barbie, Ken* and *P.J.* in the same box. *Barbie* was very current in her "Valley Girl" mini and striped socks, but the real excitement was that the box announced that *P.J.* was *Barbie's Cousin*.

214. Oscar de la Renta fashions gave Barbie a couture look once again in 1985-86. High fashion magazines even carried the ads for these gowns such as the Vogue ad shown here. 215. Peaches 'n Cream Barbie appealed to those more traditionally minded. She was also the first lead doll issued in another color besides Barbie's signature pink. Photograph courtesy of Mattel, Inc.

1984 was a big year in Barbie doll history. The company had decided to allow Barbie to be 25! In a hair color ad, Linda Evans of "Dynasty" fame proudly announced that "40 isn't fatal," and Joan Collins was a perfect size 8 at 50 years old. The baby boomers were forcing society to grow

along with them. They simply refused to give up the crown. The term "Super woman" came into being, to recognize a woman who at 35 looked perfect through diet, cosmetics and exercise and also juggled the perfect job, the perfect child and the perfect house, all without help. Glamour and glitter were at a real high. Posh new clubs were opening again, featuring music carefully called "dance" music, which was the old disco beat, jazzed up with synthesized sounds.

In 1984, on Valentine's Day in New York, Mattel sponsored a party honoring the 25th birthday of Barbie. I personally attended this party and was very surprised at all the hoopla for this event.

Selected collectors had been invited, along with Mayor Koch of NY's office, and the press. The Gallery was decorated with the new Loving You Barbie, which just happened to be dressed in white with red velvet hearts all over her dress. Tiffany silversmiths had created a statue in sterling silver of a Superstar Barbie that was valued at $50,000 and would be touring the country. Mayor Koch's assistant announced that for the rest of the day, Fifth Avenue would be renamed "Barbie Boulevard." Everyone attending received nicely done champagne glasses and napkins with "Barbie's 25th Anniversary" on them. Mattel did not care if children thought Barbie was 25. With so many top models like Cheryl Tiegs, Catherine Deneuve and Jaclyn Smith hitting 40, there seemed little to fear from being 25. How different this thinking has become in just four short years!

Other exciting dolls that year were Great Shape Barbie, Ken and Skipper who showed interest in another craze of the 1980s, AEROBICS. Developed to improve cardiovascular fitness health clubs were springing up all over the country, as people of all ages did exercises to "dance" music. It was the next movement of the roller disco fad. After one got that great body, of course, it was necessary to show it off in gowns like *Crystal Barbie* owned.

Also very worthy of mention was *Sweet Roses P.J.*, and in my opinion, the loveliest *P.J.* ever. Her gown was made like fitted rose petals, and she was scented like a rose, also. No mention of her being *Barbie's* cousin was on the box, however. *Barbie* also got a new horse, *Prancer*, who was white, (really just *Dallas*, but another color) and a little pony named *Dixie*.

Started this year was a very lovely Collectors Series of fashions, the first of which featured a holiday outfit in red velveteen, (actually available the year before for Christmas), and included a springtime ensemble and a special silver dress and cape called *Silver Sensation* which was the official 25th birthday dress. A new policy was evolving where several of next year's dolls are shown immediately after Christmas as sort of a "sneak preview" of the new line and to capture holiday money a child may have been given. In the Philadelphia area, these dolls are on the shelves the week before Christmas as well!

By 1985, the woman's movement had come full circle. Finally being a woman executive was socially acceptable. *Barbie* again, set the pace by going from a busy executive with a gold credit card, to a night on the town in *Day to Night Barbie*. Her lovely day suit and spectator pumps give way to a chic cocktail dress for night wear. Not left out were black and Hispanic *Day to Night Barbie*, as well, making another positive statement about black and Hispanic women. The Hispanic version was only sold in selected areas and will

be a great collectible in the future. Also new was *Barbie's Home and Office*, where *Barbie* could work and play.

Fashion wise, the "designer" look in American culture was never hotter. Those in the fashion world knew that a "name" on anything from sunglasses to boxer shorts meant instant sales. For 1985, Oscar de la Renta "designed" a set of four stunning gowns, very "Dynasty" inspired. Those on the inside knew that a designer at Mattel had actually made the fashions, and Oscar just approved or disapproved them. This was standard practice with all designers.

Vogue magazine ran a two-page ad showing *Barbie* dolls with clever hairstyles modeling the gowns. Even the

216. In Philadelphia, Toys Я Us had exclusive rights to these two gift sets. 1986 *Vacation Sensation* on the left, and 1985 *Dance Sensation*. 217. A selection of the *International Barbies* from the Mattel catalog for 1987. This popular series shows *Barbie* can be from any culture or race.

218. "Dynasty," one of the most popular nighttime soaps, was synonomous with glamour. *Barbie* holds her own in a breathtaking Oscar de la Renta approved gown.

219. *Tropical Barbie* and *Barbie's Island Friend, Miko*, a lovely Eurasian new friend for *Barbie*, enjoy chatting with *Tahiti*, *Barbie's* parrot.

lead doll of the year, *Peaches 'n Cream Barbie*, (who also came in black), broke tradition from "*Barbie* pink" and wore a peach chiffon gown.

A fun doll was *Dreamtime Barbie* and her bear, *BB*. Girls wanted to know that *BB* stood for. The obvious answer...*Barbie's Bear*! Dressed in a sheer nighty and robe, she was lovely.

Skipper was carefully dressed in workout gear in a gift set called *Hot Stuff Skipper*, but Mattel was very careful not to take her over the line they had crossed once with *Superteen Skipper* and *Scott*.

1986 started out very calmly with the introduction of *Magic Moves Barbie* who could move her hands through her hair. *Dream Glow Barbie* and *Ken*, dressed in almost Cinderella style,

220. For 1987, *The Rockers* were all redesigned with new fashions and hairstyles. **Ken,** with a more mature face and rooted hair, joined the group!

221. *Jewel Secrets Skipper,* new friend **Whitney, Barbie** and **Ken** are the glamorous new lead dolls for 1987. **Whitney** has super long hair. *Barbie's* life continues on into the future!

carried romanticism to new heights. What made 1986 different, forever, was the introduction of *Barbie and The Rockers.*

Rock and roll by 1986 was becoming respectible, if not patriotic, and was losing, except with some religious fanatics, its link to the drug culture. Celebrities such as Cher, Tina Turner, Bruce Springsteen and Patti Labelle denounced drugs emphatically as "uncool." Songs that had charitable purposes such as "We are the World" (which netted millions for starving worldwide), united singers from all over the world, giving rock music new respectability with parents and teachers. It did seem possible that one could

dress wildly and play loud music and still be a "decent" person. That is exactly what Mattel thought also because in a daring move, it was announced that *Barbie* would be the lead singer of a new group called, *The Rockers.* Announced in the *Barbie Drama* section of the *Barbie Magazine, Barbie* joined a group consisting of *Derek,* a Hispanic-looking boy, *Diva,* a redheaded all-American type, *Dana* an Oriental lovely and *Dee-Dee,* a black young lady. Portrayed as a struggling group with causes to conquer, they needed *Barbie* to lend her voice and support to the group.

Special Limited Edition

222. 1986 was the 100th anniversary of Sears. To celebrate, Mattel issued *Celebration Barbie,* **a fabulous doll in a pink ball gown. The collector of** *Barbie* **dolls should stock up on these specials, as they become instant collectibles when discontinued. This doll was available in retail outlets for only two months!**

With the doll came a cassette tape of songs that told it all. Titles such as "Born with a Mike in My Hand," eased parents fears that *Barbie* had gone too far again. Of course, as a spokesperson for Mattel said, there were still traditional *Barbie* dolls and outfits, such as a wedding gown, available if one found this offensive. This, again, was just ONE of the many facets of *Barbie's* never ending skills. In fact, with the addition of the *Tropical* line

of beach dolls, and *Barbie's* island friend, *Miko,* and parrot, *Tahiti,* it seemed there were plenty of personalities from which to choose in 1986!

If that was not enough, there were six more Oscar de la Renta gowns added to the Collectors Series, and more countries to the International Series. It certainly was true that *Barbie* could be whatever you wanted her to be. Unfortunately for the collector,

1986 was a banner year, but in terms of cash and space, a hard year indeed! By the end of the year, many collectors, myself included, were hoping *Barbie* would settle down just a bit, or by 1990, every closet in the house would be for *Barbie*!

Also that year was a new porcelain *Barbie* that was the start of a collectors series of dolls. Modeled after the *Superstar Barbie* and dressed in contemporary clothes, it is a nice doll and will probably be valuable in the future, but to me it is not *Barbie*. Many collectors, myself included, think of *Barbie* as vinyl and playable. The series will be continued with the next offering being a ponytail doll in *Enchanted Evening*.

Finally, 1987 saw a great new head mold for *Ken* that made him more "mature," to keep up with *Barbie's* timeless look. *Ken* also joined *The Rockers*, (probably to protect *Barbie* from *Derek*!). This year also saw the introduction of *Whitney*, a new friend with long dark hair for *Barbie*. The name, borrowed from popular singer Whitney Houston, is a highly visible name. The *Jewel Secrets* dolls, which includes *Whitney*, with clever stories, are also new for 1987.

Barbie through the 1980s has seen it all, from roller skating to aerobics; country singing to horse loving. Her ball gowns, her miniskirts, her exercise outfits and her office looks all prove the new motto so well, "We Girls Can Do Anything, Right, *Barbie*?"

As the 1980s come to a close *Barbie* will march into the 1990s and beyond, mirroring our culture as no other medium can. Through your *Barbie* doll collection, you can capture in three-dimensional form, the fads, the fancies, the good and the crazies, all through your love for *Barbie*.

223. The big news for 1986 was that *Barbie* had joined a rock group called, "The Rockers." Fashions were evolving again towards "Mod," but mixed with trash and flash! Not for every child, this *Barbie* was incredibly well received. "The Rockers" are: *Dana*, a charming Oriental, *Diva*, a devilish redhead, *Dee Dee*, a black pop star and *Derek*, a Hispanic-looking boy.

224. The Mattel catalog shows a new department store special doll for 1987, designed by Billy Boy, a New Yorker now in Paris, and called, *Feelin' Groovy Barbie*. The prudent collector will always add new and unusual versions of *Barbie* to his/her collection.

IX. Around The World With Barbie®

Just like children of each race and culture view Santa Claus as having their own characteristics, so it is with *Barbie*! One of the most rewarding and challenging parts of doll collecting is adding elusive European and other foreign items to your collection. Because of licensing agreements, these ethnically correct dolls are not available in the United States; many times, like in Japan, they are not even made by Mattel. The story of these items is indeed fascinating and a touch frustrating!

Lower airfares became a reality in the mid 1970s and opened up the entire world to many people. Some of those people just happened to be *Barbie* collectors!

One of the first "foreign" items to be found was *Barbie's Little Sister, Tutti*, a 6in (15cm) doll that had been available on the U.S. market from 1966 to 1971, but reportedly had been discontinued because of the new product safety codes. These well intended, yet severely abused codes, restricted manufacturers from making unique quality toys, and turned the responsibility for child safety over to them instead of where it belonged with the parent. As a result of these codes, a virtual "witch hunt" ensued, where

U.S. agents actually went into toy stores and removed earrings from collector dolls such as Madame Alexander's. *Tutti*, her brother, *Todd*, and friend, *Chris*, were ruled unsafe because of the wire that was molded inside the dolls to make them posable. It was believed that if one was broken (or chewed) open, an injury could result.

Collectors traveling to England in 1973 were surprised to find *Tutti, Todd* and *Chris* still on the market, only dressed and packaged differently. Recently, it has come to light that *Barbie* was sold virtually in every country around the world starting with the "Bubble Cut" dolls in the early 1960s!

Another interesting fact is that the quality is much better for most foreign products. The accessories are more realistic, the clothing better made, and many times even the theme of the doll itself is more imaginative than a lot of the U.S. marketed items.

225. Imagine! Who would ever think in 1959 that *Barbie* would be seen like this! *Rocker Barbie* from Rio de Janeiro, Brazil, 1986. Her quality is fantastic, with thick curly rooted purple afro and jointed wrists. Made under license by Estrella Company.

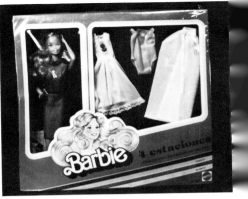

Several reasons can be cited for this, the main one being that the rest of the world is really a two-class society, that of rich and poor, where the United States is made up a large middle class with about 20% of the population labeled as "rich or poor." In the U.S., Mattel aims *Barbie* mainly at this middle class, who for the most part view a toy as something you give a child to play with until it breaks, then replace it with something new. This is a relatively new attitude in this country, as "disposable" everything is a recent phenomenon. In most foreign countries, children are like they were here in the 1950s, whereby a child is given lovely things and taught to take care of them.

Also adding to this quality gap is that Americans consider their job a source of income to pay for their lifestyle, where in other countries, pride in one's work as a craftsman is still a means in itself. In all fairness, labor is cheap in some foreign countries and

226. 1976 *Gold Medal Barbie* from Australia. Issued worldwide for the Olympics, the design of her gold medal even included a kangaroo!

227. Mexico had wonderful gift sets! This 1981 set is titled *4 Estaciones* (4 seasons), and features a darker-skinned doll with four outfits.

this, too, widens the quality gulf for the collector.

In 1968, Elliot Handler stated that Mattel products were sold in over 60 countries. *Barbie* Fan Club members have been reported in such unlikely places as Zambia, Guam, Saudi Arabia, Cyprus, Turkey and New Zealand. The collector of these items would do well (and save much money) to make friends with airline personnel, for that seems to be the richest source of foreign *Barbie* items in the U.S.

The countries that produce the most interesting items seem to be those in which the American standard of beauty is idealized. In Japan, for example, the "preppie" look is still worshipped, and the Sandra Dee, Troy Donahue, blonde, blue-eyed standard is very much on a pedestal. Of course, like looking at a travel brochure of a city, these people have a media-induced view of American life that does not include crime, poverty or ghettos. What they see in news reports or in rock videos is what we WANT them to see, and like looking into a fishbowl, one does not view the entire ocean!

Many countries, like Australia, have pictured *Barbie* in pith helmet and safari gear. Ireland, long the land of shamrocks, has used green as the official color of *Great Shape Barbie*, depicted here in "aerobic teal blue."

Names are often changed of successful dolls to the resort of the particular country, as in *Malibu Barbie*, which is listed as *Saint Tropez Barbie* in French speaking countries and *Portofino Barbie* in Italian markets.

Health laws, again well intended but misdirected, also affect quality in European products. *Barbie's Horse, Dallas* and *Western Barbie* are real examples of the quality gap. The European version of *Dallas* is fully-jointed, like the *Dancer* horse of the early

228

229

228. The Estrella Company, now no longer a Mattel license, made some wonderful dolls in the 1980s. This doll, with top quality jointed wrists and many accessories, is called *The Beautiful One Who Is a Star*. 229. *Barbie 5th Anniversary Gift Set* from Spain. This gorgeous set from 1985 features a fabulous doll with dark skin and platinum hair. The quality of the doll is outstanding but the extra clothes are poorly made.

131

1970s made for the U.S. market. His mane is even real horse hair, which would be outlawed here. *Western Barbie* comes with an extra outfit and features jointed arms and the "busy" hands which open and close and were part of the early 1970s line. The dolls cost much more in these foreign markets (almost double), but are aimed at a higher audience than the American doll. To doll collectors, it is very reminiscent of Madame Alexander dolls here in this country which are directed at the upper class.

Particularly of note were the gorgeous dolls made by the Takara Company in Japan, under license from Mattel, which were unbelievably well made. Photography in the catalogs rivaled the finest fashion magazines, and many times the lifelike quality of the dolls is uncanny. Modeled after the old "Speed Racer" cartoons, the dolls have big round eyes highlighted with three slash lines at the outer corners and silky blonde hair. The Oriental race must see our eyes as huge and round, for all the cartoons and dolls out of Japan have the same shape to the eyes.

The life-style of *Barbie* and *Ken* in Japan again depicts college life with the idealized standard of an outsider looking in at only what the "Chamber

230. Canada, right across our borders, has always been a rich source for unusual *Barbie* dolls. From left, *Hawaiian Superstar Barbie*, 1978; *Picture Pretty Barbie*, 1978; *Fabulous Fur Barbie*, 1985; and *Partytime Barbie*, available in two faces, 1977. 231. Mattel claimed that *Barbie* was not sold in Japan in the late 1970s, but this great gift set featuring a *Superstar Barbie* and her *Starcycle* was bought there in 1978!

of Commerce" wants you to see, and depicts *Barbie* much the same way as she was in the early 1960s here.

Recently a new company, Bandai, in Japan, received the Mattel license and combined with them to form "MA-BA" (Mattel-Bandai), to make new creations. Mattel seems interested in scaling down the creative aspects of *Barbie* as these new dolls lack the realism and imagination of the Takara dolls. Takara, on the other hand, continued using all their old ideas in a new doll called *Jenny* which is a collectible in itself, but is not at all tied into *Barbie*.

In France, a doll of a French country singer in the early 1980s joined the *Barbie* family, in the guise of *Chantal Goya*. The doll was billed as "being able to wear *Barbie's* lovely fashions," and followed the pattern started with *Julia* here in the U.S., where a licensed "friend," as it were, was able to share *Barbie's* bountiful wardrobe!

Canada has also been a source of *Barbie* dolls with creative themes.

---

232. The pride and joy of any *Barbie* collection are the foreign items that show *Barbie* as she appears to that culture. This very rare *Hundslade* (hound sled), was offered in 1981 for the Scandanavian countries. The doll is the beautiful *Snoprinsessa Barbie* (*Snow Princess Barbie*) that pictures *Barbie* in the land of the midnight sun.

Hawaiian Superstar Barbie used the Superstar molds in ethnic fashion before the U.S. did, and each year the Canadian market gets a "set" of *Barbie* and *Ken* with a theme, such as 1987s *Tennis Barbie* and *Tennis Ken*. The strange thing is that almost without fail, the accompanying *Skipper* doll that matches the set, and is even shown on the box, is not sold in Canada, but is available only in England, France, Italy and Germany! No explanation for this is ever given, and has frustrated many a collector when visiting Canada to buy the latest *Barbie* dolls.

---

233. Booklet from Japan, 1969, showing *Barbie's* friend, *Living Eli*. This is the rarest of all the *Barbie* friends. Interestingly, her face mold showed up in the U.S. on a cheaply made doll Mattel made for discount stores called *Sweet 16*.

234

235

234. One of the most beautiful sets ever made for *Barbie* was this *Equestrienne Barbie and Her Horse, Dancer,* sold in Canada, 1977. The doll was the old *Barbie* face with rooted eyelashes, not seen in years in the U.S., and *Dancer* was fully-jointed.

236

235. American native Billy Boy persuaded Mattel, France, to make this edition of *Barbie* in 1985. Billy Boy sees *Barbie* here as his "dream girl," and dresses her as such. This doll was part of a display that toured the U.S. featuring designer gowns for *Barbie*.

236. Germany has long been a source of great *Barbie* treasures. 1986 saw these great *Music Lovin' Barbie, Ken* and *Skipper* offered for sale. As usual, the *Ken* and *Barbie* were available in Canada, but not the *Skipper*! No explanation of this has been found!

237

237. The Takara Company of Japan had the most famous license in Mattel history. Producing dolls that were perfect miniatures of American life, they did their job so well, they threatened domestic sales as so many dolls were imported illegally. They lost their license in 1986. This set of *Barbie* and *Ken* show American teenagers as seen through the eyes of the Japanese.

Also of note is that *Ken* is often dressed in outfits that here would draw stares as being too "high fashion" for middle class American men not as style conscious as their European counterparts.

Other interesting comments on foreign *Barbie* items include the mention that all Mexican dolls are darker skinned, with "bleached" looking blonde hair. More noteworthy, however, is the fact that so many of the Mexican dolls were being brought across the border by doll dealers to sell here, that the government made the factory shrink wrap ALL *Barbie* dolls to prevent drug smuggling in the doll boxes!

In Spain, again *Barbie* is made with darker skin but has incredibly fine, platinum blonde hair that seems not to match her skin tones, but implies "dye job," or "movie star hair." The quality of the doll made for Spain is again better than the U.S. dolls, but the clothing quality is not as nice.

238. The "swan song" of Takara was this *Mink Barbie*, featuring *Barbie* in a designer dress and real ranch mink coat. The styling of the case and the stand were first class. It is sad that dolls like this are not offered on the U.S. market!

239. In 1986, Mattel combined forces with a Japanese company, Bandai, to form MA-BA. Mattel wanted closer control over the Japanese products. The MA-BA *Barbie* and *Ken* are nice, but lack the imagination of the Takara dolls. Takara has recently won a lawsuit against the Bandai company for using their basic mold ideas.

One should mention also that almost all Mattel dolls are currently made either in the Phillipines, Taiwan, Malaysia or Hong Kong. The Phillipines manufactured dolls appear first in the stores and are not the quality of those made by the other factories. Often they are "orange" in skin tone, with pale, washed out makeup. On the lead doll for 1987, *Jewel Secrets Barbie*, even those manufacturered for the European markets had a sickly orange cast to them with little makeup.

Brazil was just recently one of the best places to buy unique, different *Barbie* dolls, made under license by the Estrella Company, but collectors traveling there in February 1987, were told that the company had surrendered their license. Their ideas were wonderful, and often used old molds they must have obtained from Mattel at some point, as packaged with the dolls were items not sold here in years, such as little curling irons and barrettes.

---

240. *Barbie* by the Takara Company in Japan was seen as having big eyes and blonde hair. She came dressed in the traditional kimono, and as *Romantic Barbie* on the right.

241. The richness of the Takara gift sets was like something made here in the 1950s. Fabulous satin dresses, fur coats and minute accessories made *Barbie* come alive. This set made for Christmas 1985, featured *Barbie* photographs that were like studio portraits! Lucky is the collector who has these sets!

242. Designer tie-ins for the Takara *Barbie* like this coordinating set made by Kansai, rivaled Bloomingdale's displays! This set is light years ahead of the American *Barbie* fashions.

The Scandinavian countries also have produced some great items such as *Snow Princess Barbie*, depicting *Barbie* with the fine dark hair and pale skin of those not exposed to harsh sunlight further south.

It is safe to say that the collector of *Barbie* dolls can assemble a veritable smorgasbord of dolls from around the world that represent *Barbie* with almost every racial feature imaginable. This is as it should be, and a sign that we are moving into some enlightenment, at least, where people are satisfied with who and what they are, rather than wishing to be some idealized standard. By viewing a strong, independent character such as *Barbie*, who CAN do anything, and really has been successful, (and is their own race), a child strengthens his/her own self-esteem. Through playing with a *Barbie* doll that represents that child's race, egos are enhanced and even relations with the U.S. improve. For too long Americans have had a negative image abroad and now that situation is being helped by, of all things, *Barbie*!

Truly, the collector of *Barbie* dolls around the world cannot help broaden his/her perspective as well, and learn to appreciate ALL cultures worldwide. For the collector who likes to specialize, these elusive foreign dolls make a challenging hobby, and one that adds to peace and contentment in world relations. A trip around the world with *Barbie* is indeed a wise investment!

243. In 1986, Takara borrowed the original ponytail molds from Mattel and produced these fantastic dolls, dressed by designer Hiomichi Nakano. Simply called *American Doll*, they were as well made as the American dolls of the 1960s.

244. PB, a department store in Japan, convinced Mattel and Bandai to reissue the old faces from the 1960s. These outstanding dolls are made from the old ponytail, bubble cut, and twist and turn faces. The clothing is either reproductions of older outfits, or as shown here, original designs. The logo shown is *Barbie* as was seen in the 1960s!

X. Tammy®. The Doll You Love...To Dress

The registered trademarks, the trademarks and the copyrights appearing in italics within this chapter belong to Mattel, Inc., unless otherwise noted.

By 1961, the popularity of *Barbie* was well established. Every major and minor manufacturer had entered the teen fashion doll race. The truth was the market was so large AND so popular that there was room for all. The face of the doll market (and society) had changed much, from emphasis on the child, to catering to the teenage market; everyone was making money off the miniature teen fashion doll craze. The boom children refused to let go of the attention of the nation (a trait they still possess as today women over 40 dominate the fashion and entertainment field).

Some executives of toy companies and parents still felt in 1961 that *Barbie* was too sexy and "over-developed." Also, the baby boom had lasted so long that there still were hoards of younger children coming up. Like waves on the ocean, these children, now in elementary school, kept filling up the homes and schools of America. Not having been raised on the Marilyn Monroe type of glamour, these pre-teens could perhaps be "soft peddled" slightly on the role sophistication would play in their lives.

The Ideal Toy Corp., long famous for making money off their child star dolls, felt now was the time to act. In 1962, they issued *Tammy, The Doll You Love...To Dress*. Not as old as *Barbie*, nor as shapely, *Tammy* seemed a bit less threatening to the values of the day. Minus, too, was the presence of a boyfriend. In fact, *Tammy* had a complete family that consisted in her height of popularity of *Mom, Dad,* brother *Ted,* little sister *Pepper, Dodi,* a friend of *Pepper's* and little brother *Pete.* Opposite to *Barbie, Tammy's* friends seemed to be "racier" than *Tammy* herself. Friend *Glamour Misty* wore silver glitter outfits that were far more sophisticated than *Tammy's* image; the *Miss Clairol Doll,* made from the same molds bleached her hair in shocking colors.

All in all, the glamous image that many moralists found offensive was missing in *Tammy.* Ideal specifically designed her to be 12in (30cm) tall so that she could not be in scale to *Barbie.* For the most part, the fashions between the two dolls were not interchangeable,

249. By 1964, *Tammy* had been allowed to grow up slightly. New *Posn' Tammy* sported an American Girl hairdo just like *Barbie* and wore couture inspired clothing.

Tammy®, Mom®, Dad®, Ted®, Pepper®, Dodi®, Pete®, Glamour Misty®, Posn' Tammy® and *Miss Clairol®,* are registered trademarks of the Ideal Toy Corp.

245. *Tammy, The Doll You Love...To Dress,* dressed as Queen of the Prom. **246.** Debbie Reynolds in her role as Tammy. Produced by Ross Hunter, the Tammy movies, starring Reynolds and Sandra Dee, tied in the down-to-earth image of the American family. *Movie Star News photograph.*

Tammy®, Picnic Party®, Beau and Arrow®, Sorority Sweetheart® and *School Daze®* are registered trademarks of the Ideal Toy Corp.

Clever outfits such as *Picnic Party* and *Beau and Arrow* were designed with amazing attention to detail. *Sorority Sweetheart* and *School Daze* all told the story of an ORDINARY girl's high school life. This was at the heart of the difference between *Tammy* and *Barbie*. *Tammy* was just an average schoolgirl like those of the TV sitcoms of the day. *Barbie* was a globe-trotting high fashion model that was so perfect that reality was stretched almost beyond the beliefs of many simple American children.

The three or four years separating this current 1962 generation of pre-teens and those ahead of them was surprisingly eventful. A movie producer, Ross Hunter, in the late 1950s believed that movies could capture once again the audience lost to television if only GLAMOUR was reintroduced. The gorgeous "women's pictures" of the 1930s, such as *The Women*, were indeed gone from the screen. With *Imitation of Life, Portrait in Black* and *Backstreet*, Hunter lured the "costume" effect back into fashion. Spawned during this period, *Barbie* mirrored the fantasy projection of a woman-child traveling the world of glamour. The next group of teens had missed out on this entirely and saw *Tammy* as a more down-to-earth role model. Even Mattel lessened *Barbie's* sophistication by 1964, when her careers centered more around her college days than her modeling talents.

The other concept behind *Tammy* was one of the American family. *Barbie*

meaning the owner of *Tammy* had to purchase a separate wardrobe. The same tie-in concept with other products was tried, however, as *Tammy* had storybooks, paper dolls, record albums and dozens of licensed products.

The clothing itself was stunning and just as well made as the *Barbie* fashions. Many *Barbie* collectors today consider themselves "traitors" to collect other fashion dolls, but like the macho man who has learned that sensitivity is a blessing, *Barbie* collectors are discovering other dolls that tell the fashion story as well as *Barbie*.

247. The less developed figure of *Tammy*, and her school girl image, made her one of the most popular teen fashion dolls ever. Storybooks were available of her down home adventures.
248. *Glamour Misty*, *Tammy's* racy friend, came in a phone booth. Her outfit, a silver lame jumpsuit, was a far cry from *Tammy's* earlier image. With her "flip" hairdo, she had much more personality than *Tammy* herself.

had been just three years too soon to benefit from the all-American image that the family had in the early 1960s. Shows like "Ozzie and Harriet," and the aforementioned "The Donna Reed Show" and "Father Knows Best," all portrayed a stereotyped image of the American family that even today is regarded by many to be the ideal. This type of family, perfect in every way, became almost a neurotic obsession for many of the period; a fantasy that has sent many a woman to the psychiatrist's couch trying to figure out how to dust curtain rods and bake cookies at the same time while still looking "crinoline crisp" with a string of pearls!

Tammy had come along at just the correct time. In 1963 Ideal issued dolls representing her father, called appropriately *Dad*, brother *Ted* (who shared the same Ivy League wardrobe), and, of course, *Mom*, whose outfits consisted mainly of housedresses to care for her family, and an occasional "evening gown" for that special yearly night out. In fact, that was the dilemma of the American teen by 1963. The life they led was so much fun, so chock full of activities and self-exploration that many would find "settling down" a prospect not to be considered until decades later.

As the popularity of *Tammy* increased, Mattel responded by "taming

down" *Barbie*. By the mid-1960s, both dolls sported "American Girl" hairdos and wore couture clothes. It was this "equality" that spelled the end for the *Tammy* saga. Mattel was known for its uncanny ability to predict which direction society was moving (a trait they still possess today). *Barbie* was outselling *Tammy* drastically. The final "blow" came when the British Invasion occurred in 1965. Ideal was simply not geared financially to redesign the *Tammy* "All American" concept as Mattel did with *Barbie*. Suddenly American teens no longer looked to their own country for their image. Like a clock ticking backwards 200 years, England and the Beatles took "the colonies" by storm. *Tammy* died a graceful death, like Mary Stone on "The Donna Reed Show." *Barbie*, MODified and updated, moved on. The race was over and *Barbie* had won. The collector of teen fashion dolls was really the winner, for today, *Tammy*, *The Doll You Love...To Dress*, is now a doll you love to collect!

Tammy®, *Glamour Misty*®, *Dad*®, *Ted*® and *Mom*® are registered trademarks of the Ideal Toy Corp.

XI. Tressy® And Judy Littlechap®...

The registered trademarks, the trademarks and the copyrights appearing in italics within this chapter belong to Mattel, Inc., unless otherwise noted.

In 1963, more contenders entered the lucrative teen fashion doll race. By this time, *Barbie* was selling at the rate of over six million dolls a year! Mattel was the largest manufacturer of ladies clothing in the world; it just was doll size. The arrival of *Fashion Queen Barbie* with her three wigs began a few years of hair play emphasis. One doll that entered the race rose to the place of real competition. Her name was *Tressy*.

The American Character Doll Co. was no stranger to fashion dolls. Having secured the *Toni* license from The Gillette Company when Ideal tired of it, this firm issued gorgeous high heel fashion dolls bearing the *Toni* name. It is interesting to note how the *Toni* doll had grown along with the boom children, from a toddler image of the present, to the future image of sophistication. The company also issued the same doll as *Sweet Sue Sophisticate*. Equipped with a bra and nylons, she came in the demure size of 10in (25cm) and definitely was a forerunner of *Barbie*.

Tressy had a magic feature that both *Tammy* and *Barbie* lacked. Her hair "grew!" A long strand of hair could be pulled out of the top of her head. A brass key in the shape of a "T" was inserted in her back to rewind the "secret strand," as it was called. The rest of *Tressy's* hair was one length to her chin. The styling possibilities were endless. American Character, known for their quality dolls, had a winner. Her fashions, however, left much to be desired, but American Character dolls were not known for their clothing, but for their rich, heavy vinyl.

Like the other fashion dolls, *Tressy* was available in a wide range of hair colors. The missing element in her story, however, was any kind of personality. *Tressy* was just another teenage girl who was pretty and had lots of wonderful clothes. Actually, she cost $4.98 in 1963, which was more than the other fashion dolls did, but the growing hair feature warranted this higher price.

250. American Character's *Tressy*® sports a 1960s "Beehive" hairstyle. Included with the doll was a fashion booklet, shown right. The *Tressy's* Hair Glamour book, published by Dell, showed all *Tressy's*® hairstyle fashions.

Tammy® is a registered trademark of the Ideal Toy Corp.

Tressy® and *Sweet Sue Sophisticate*® are registered trademarks of the American Character Doll Co.
Toni® is a registered trademark of The Gillette Co.   *Judy Littlechap* is a registered trademark of Remco Industries.

By 1965, *Tressy* had gained a little sister, *Cricket*, who also had the grow hair feature and a "best friend," *Mary Make-Up*. Like with all fashion dolls, the term "best friend" implied that both dolls were the same size and able to share clothing.

Collectors of teen fashion dolls often overlook the *Tressy* wardrobe, mainly because it is so difficult to find mint-in-box. These outfits are very unique, with themes that add so much to the study of 1960s pop culture. Outfits such as *Hooray! Hootenanny Tonight* told of the country singing so popular in 1963, and *Party of the Year!*, where *Tressy* becomes "Miss American Character," giving her real status as a winner. Because these outfits were not as plentiful as *Tammy's* or *Barbie's*, they are very difficult to find today. A complete MIB collection of them is quite rare and if the demand were higher, would command much more than *Barbie* clothing would.

The hair play aspect of *Tressy* became so popular that in 1965, Dell Publishers made a little "pocket book" of hairstyles that could be done for *Tressy*. Folks may fondly remember the little Dell books that were available in the checkout line at the supermarket on subjects that ranged from diets to dog care. *Tressy's Hair Glamour* was such a publication and is a real period piece to fans of hairstyles. Complete instructions were given to construct such enduring styles as "Beach Beauty Bob," a sleek pageboy, or "World's Fairest Do," a flip with top braid to wear to the New York World's Fair! Other teen dream styles included "Royal Pouf," a jeweled upsweep, and, of course, a "Beehive Bubble" to wear to a "pink champagne ball."

Tressy was what today psychologists call a "conspicuous consumer," for she definitely reveled in the status symbols of the day. No visible means of support was offered for her life-style, and in my opinion, this was really the missing element that led to her demise.

In 1965, *Mary Make-Up*, *Tressy* and *Cricket* all came in gift sets with hair color or hair play accessories. *Tressy* also had her own apartment "for gracious living," which led the more astute child to wonder just who "kept" *Tressy* in the life-style to which she had become accustomed. Her age seemed a mystery as well, but few 16-year-olds could be living on their own in a penthouse. This year was the last year *Tressy* and her world were offered. 1966 showed no listing for these dolls in most catalogs.

Perhaps *Tressy's* family or whomever had gotten tired of supporting her...maybe she married and left town, but for whatever reason, *Tressy* was gone. The collector of this doll has a real job to do, for *Tressy*, her friends and her fashions are the most difficult to find of all the teen fashion dolls. Fortunate is the collector who has been foresighted enough to collect these dolls. I predict that *Tressy* has a great future as a collectible!

---

251. The *Littlechap Family* by Remco Industries idealized the upper class American family. Daughter *Judy* was the "wealthiest" of all the fashion doll princesses!

Tressy®, Cricket®, Mary Make-Up®, Hooray! Hootenanny Tonight® and Party of the Year® are all registered trademarks of the American Character Doll Co.
Tammy® is a registered trademark of the Ideal Toy Corp.

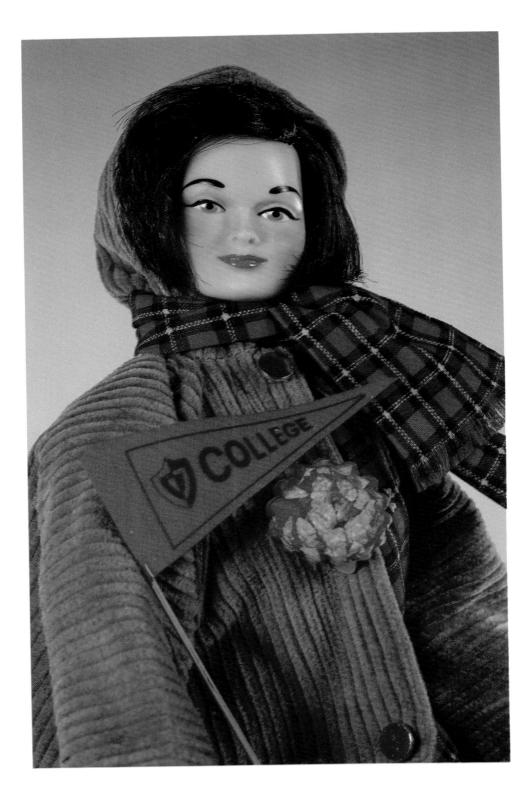

Naturally, the *Barbie* doll story must be the longest tale of the fashion doll saga because of *Barbie's* 30 years of existence. Other dolls of one or two years duration can tell us just as much about the slice of life they represent.

Judy Littlechap is such a doll. The largest of the teen fashion dolls, 13½in (35cm), her story is also the grandest. Remco Industries was a stranger to the doll business. They were best known for boys' toys with an action theme. Perhaps this is why they could enter the fashion doll race with, in my opinion, the most imaginative of all the teen fashion dolls.

On the drawing boards in 1962, the *Littlechap Family* did not make its appearance into the toy stores until 1964. The family made no apologies about being upper class. The slice of life they offered was one of perfection and stability. The father of the family, *Dr. John Littlechap*, was described as having "a masculine movie star physique, graying at the temples." His accomplishments in the booklet that accompanied all the dolls and outfits listed him as "a member of the Lanesville County Medical Society, former Flight Surgeon U.S. Army Air Force... and loves his family and golf."

Naturally anyone that wonderful would have an equally outstanding wife. *Lisa Littlechap*, elegantly coiffed in a "beehive" that had streaks of gray, was "a former model, wonderful cook...president of the P.T.A., and the best dressed woman in town."

Their two daughters were, naturally, highly motivated and the kind of daughters one would expect a doctor and his wife to have. *Libby Littlechap*, kid sister of the family was, "age 10, fifth grader at Lanesville Elementary School...loves to climb trees, pester her sister, and wants to be a doctor like her daddy." (Of course, this was only a hero worship dream, as her destiny more than likely would be changing drapes in her gorgeous home than changing uniforms).

The eldest daughter, *Judy Littlechap*, was the "big sister" of the *Littlechap Family*. Described as "age 17, honor student at Lanesville High, she loved parties and crazy desserts." Two kinds of children seemed to enjoy playing with the *Littlechap Family*---those who lived the very life they represented and those who wished they did. Children are, in my opinion, much more astute than adults give them credit for, and many a little girl saw herself in *Judy Littlechap*, or the self that she longed to be. Whatever the reason, *Judy Littlechap* was a quality doll with an uncanny resemblance to Jacqueline Kennedy. Many novice doll collectors often think that the *Judy Littlechap* doll is a portrait doll of Mrs. Kennedy. Indeed, the message of grace and class is the same. The *Littlechaps* behaved "correctly," and were the epitome of the upstanding family of the time.

The collector of these dolls does not have too difficult a time amassing a

---

252. *Judy Littlechap*® wears *Judy's Football Outfit*®, 1964. Naturally, a well bred young lady like *Judy* would attend all the "right" games and, of course, wore Princeton colors and a mum, as was the custom.

Judy Littlechap® *Littlechap Family*®, *Dr. John Littlechap*®, *Lisa Littlechap*® and *Libby Littlechap*® are all registered trademarks of Remco Industries.

mint-in-box collection. The dolls did not sell well and much old store stock has remained. When researching this section of the book, this author was able quite easily to obtain every outfit ever made for *Judy Littlechap* mint in the box within a period of 30 days. This availablility gives a false impression, however, that interest or quality is lacking. Fashion doll collectors are turning to the other dolls from the past 30 years that represent the history of fashion and pop culture. These outfits will soon disappear into the collections of the astute collector, raising the prices on them to the level they should be for something so nice that is from 1964.

My theory of why the dolls were not a success is based on several facts. It is only today, when we look backward at the dolls and their outfits, that we see the brilliant social statement they make. Our quest for "nostalgia" (which is to me a longing to have again something you took for granted at the time) plus our added knowledge about sociology and even fashion, make the owner of the *Littlechap Family* wish life could again be that simple. What did *Judy Littlechap* know of poverty, crime or despair? Her life as the daughter of a wealthy doctor shielded her from contact with any of life's unpleasantnesses. Collectors today are desirous of all these statements the doll makes.

In 1964, however, who knew that the assassinations of leaders, the Vietnam War and the drug culture lay just ahead to disturb the peace! The *Littlechaps* must be viewed with 1960s eyes to make a critical judgment. The truth is that the dolls were AWKWARD. Limbs were too long, feet turned out at angles, faces devoid of character...all

these led to the rapid demise of this family of dolls.

Today, older and wiser, the *Littlechap Family* is remembered more for what it says about our ideas of perfection in 1964 than our standards of workmanship. The psychological and sociological message of many modern dolls is the REAL appeal to most collectors. Those who do not feel this often find the attraction to these dolls strange as they are judging them on quality alone. To those who collect them, teen fashion dolls are a three-dimensional textbook of America as we would like to remember it.

OPPOSITE PAGE: The upper class family known as the *Littlechaps*, here described ever so "properly" on the back of their wardrobe boxes.

Judy Littlechap® and *Littlechap Family*® are registered trademarks of Remco Industries.

The *Littlechap* Family

Meet the Littlechap family: Dr. John Littlechap; Lisa, his wife; their two daughters — 17 year old Judith and 10 year old Libby.

Never before has a family of dolls been created that is so true to life. Be sure to see and buy them at your favorite toy store.

Judith Littlechap
friends call her Judy — age 17 — honor student at Lanesville High School — Senior class — loves parties and crazy desserts.

Libby Littlechap
age 10 — fifth grader at Lanesville Elementary School — loves to climb trees. pester her sister, and wants to be a doctor like her Daddy.

Lisa Littlechap
attractive mother of Judith and Libby — former model — wonderful cook — President of the P.T.A., and best-dressed woman in town.

Dr. John Littlechap
member of the Lanesville County Medical Society — former flight surgeon U. S. Army Air Force — loves his family and golf — wishes he could find more time for both.

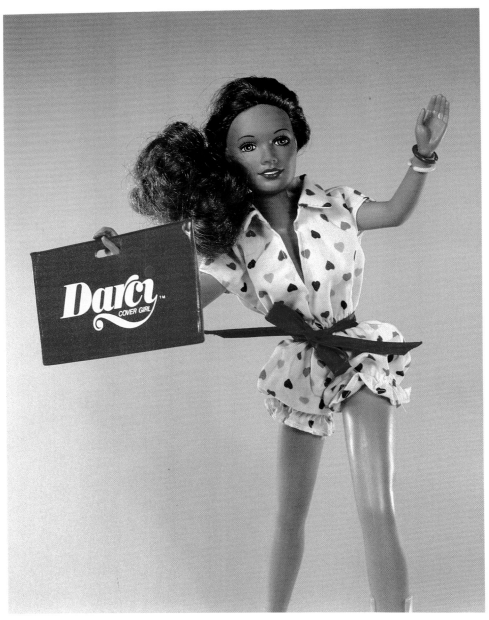

253. Kenner's *Darci*® was the outstanding fashion doll of the late 1970s.

XII. Et Al...

It would be an impossible goal to list all the teen fashion dolls of the past 30 years. Even more impossible would it be to illustrate all the thousands of fashions made for them. This genre of doll, born really in the late 1950s, is still the mainstay of the doll industry. Dolls have come and gone, some so generic and cheaply made that they are not worthy of mention. Others have been wonderful, and quite frankly overlooked by teen fashion doll collectors. Any successful product is going to be copied. Imitation is the sincerest form of flattery. Like *Barbie* took the teen fashion dolls of the 1950s one step further, some other dolls since 1959 also have made brilliant statements of our culture.

Unfortunately for the doll collector, money was usually the motivator behind the release of any doll. A company is in business to show a profit. Usually there are stockholders to answer to, bills to be paid; the more popular dolls produce more money. As any viewer of television who has had a favorite series canceled can tell you, the most popular is not always the best! Like Nielsen ratings determine which shows get the ax, so do financial reports determine which dolls remain and which ones are discontinued.

This is why the fashion doll collector would do well to add currently available dolls to their collections that appeal to them when they see them. When sales dip, or never take off, these items rapidly disappear. If a company declares bankruptcy, inventory is sometimes taken right off the shelves! Just like a television viewer would be wise to tape a treasured program lest it never be seen again, so should the doll collector buy on sight those items which appeal to them. The words "popular," and "esthetic" are NOT the same, and many good dolls such as Kenner's *Darci* were of unbelievable quality, but for some reason did not appeal to the masses. Also, when collecting play dolls that are in reality designed for young children (the age of playing with dolls is lower than it was in 1959), what is attractive to you as an adult collector might be above the level necessary for the doll to succeed as a child's toy.

Sometimes the opposite spells the demise of a doll. Even the prestigious Alexander Doll Co., Inc., felt obligated to enter the teen fashion doll race. In fact, so committed were they that their entry, *Brenda Starr*, was the "cover girl" on their 1964 catalog. Advertised

Darci® is a registered trademark of Kenner.

Brenda Starr is a registered trademark of the Alexander Doll Co., Inc.

in the catalog (Alexander dolls were never on television, much too vulgar a medium) as "different from any other doll of this type, of a finely finished high grade of plastic," the doll also featured sleep eyes and a rooted non-retractable long strand of hair like *Tressy's*. Naturally what made *Brenda Starr* worthy of competing was that her fashions were made with the Alexander magic touch of high quality.

The company hoped that mothers and daughters, seeing the obvious high quality of *Brenda Starr*, sold only in "better" stores, would buy her instead of *Barbie*. They were wrong. The age of the wealthy child living in a vacuum was over, thanks to television, and TV was where *Barbie* was making it big. Despite the fact that *Brenda Starr* WAS the high quality doll she claimed to be, and even though she came in exquisitely packaged gift sets, little girls were mesmerized by *Barbie* in 1964, much the same way children were by *Cabbage Patch Kids* dolls in 1983.

Finally in 1965, deciding probably that paying extra for the *Brenda Starr* license was making no difference in sales, Alexander issued the exact same doll and called her *Yolanda*. Available only in 1965, *Yolanda* is fantastic and another doll that is often overlooked by teen fashion doll collectors. Offered as a bride, she was stunning. Also issued was a heavy satin formal with sequin-trimmed bodice and a gorgeous

254. *Brenda Starr*® **was Madame Alexander's entry into the fashion doll contest in 1964. A lovely high quality doll, she did not catch on with the public. 255. Kenner issued** *Dusty*® **in 1974. Overly athletic and not very feminine, she was rapidly discontinued.**

pleated tulle formal with roses in her hair.

The obvious answer to why a doll is discontinued is because it is not selling well. *Brenda Starr* and *Yolanda* will be remembered as the "rich man's *Barbie*." Even today, when most Alexander dolls from that period are bringing fantastic sums when mint, these dolls have not risen in value like others have. The dolls, like a wonderful TV movie, disappeared, never to be seen again.

Doll companies were having so much trouble competing with *Barbie* that most major manufacturers just gave up. For the rest of the 1960s, and on into the early 1970s, there was not a serious challenger for a piece of the fashion doll pie. Naturally, at the supermarket or drug store one could still see in plastic bags the blank-faced cheaply made teen fashion doll imitators, but a real doll with an image, a name and a personality was simply not worth the trouble.

Finally in the early 1970s, a breakthrough occurred. As discussed in a previous chapter, Mattel had gone through a traumatic leadership and financial period. All this had taken its toll dramatically on the dolls. By 1973, *Barbie* dolls were available that, in my opinion, were not much better than the dime store dolls competing with them.

Some toy companies saw this as opportunity knocking. Here was the first real chance in almost 15 years to "dethrone" *Barbie*, the queen of teen fashion dolls. The women's movement was in full swing. Athletes like Billy Jean King were telling women that the best way to compete in a man's world was aggressively. Suddenly the movement for some went to extreme. Masculine looking women, with chopped hairstyes, seemed to overtake the

256. LJN's *Brooke Shields, The World's Most Glamourous Teenage Doll*. A stunningly realistic portrait doll, this challenger sold quite well in 1982 and 1983.

glamourous ones. Some women began to question why they were spending hours on makeup and hair. Was it to please themselves, or men, which were being viewed as oppressive by the mid 1970s.

In 1974, Kenner issued *Dusty*, a robust, athletic girl doll that was a sports figure. Her size was 12in (30cm), and she could not fit in *Barbie* clothes, not that she would have wanted to! *Dusty* and black girlfriend, *Skye*, for some mothers gave their daughters a chance at something more than a beauty parlour life. Little girls were involved in lawsuits to be allowed to play on boys' sports teams. Like other minorities, the pendulum of their desires would swing too far, then settle back again. For now, some feminists saw *Dusty* as the perfect rebellion against the glamour image. The public, however, saw things differently. Not

Dusty® and *Skye*® are registered trademarks of Kenner.

Brooke Shields® is a registered trademark of LJN Toys, Ltd.

257. The 1980s has opened up the world of rock star fashion dolls. Creata has introduced *Lace*®, an exciting rock band that features wild fashions. The dolls are unnamed, adding to play value.

Lace® is a registered trademark of Creata.

to be used as pawns, little girls who not yet faced sex discrimination seemed not as interested in proving a point as did their mothers. Mattel quickly got their problems straightened out, and Kenner learned that *Dusty* was not the answer to the long run that *Barbie* had enjoyed. The mistake they made, in my opinion, is that *Barbie* has been kept current, BUT feminine. Like "Charlie's Angels," *Barbie* did not sacrifice glamour for adventure. Little girls seemed to agree, for *Dusty* "hit

the dust" after a brief run. Kenner was not ready to give up, however.

As previously discussed, the late 1970s saw the birth of the club culture. Dressing up, disco dancing and going out were the new American pastimes. Glamour was back more than ever, and Kenner again entered the fashion doll race with one of the finest products ever produced.

In 1978, *Darci* was introduced. A top fashion model AND cover girl, *Darci* was a high quality, 12in (30cm) doll that had setable nylon hair that was fully-rooted and very stylable, with a wardrobe of up-to-the-minute fashions. *Darci*, as a blonde, brunette or redhead, lived the "Charlie's Angels" type of life that was so popular. The doll was simply stunning. A beautiful store display captured the

Darci® and *Dusty*® are registered trademarks of Kenner.

attention of the buying public. *Darci* was the embodiment of all that American women stood for. Beautiful, sophisticated, independent, talented and athletic, *Darci* had a strong, but feminine personality. A friend, *Erica*, was added to the line, as well as *Dana*, *Darci's* counterpart in black. Lucky is the collector who has put away these fine dolls, for they are truly lovely and of the finest quality. Each outfit came with a small cover of a magazine such as *New Woman*, *Bride's Magazine* or *Disco Scene* that featured *Darci* on the cover.

Added to the line was a van which *Darci* drove herself to her location shots, a modeling studio that had working lights, and a Disco, which she designed herself, and owned and operated. *Darci* was a positive role model for any young girl who saw herself as wanting to get involved with life. No mention of a boyfriend or future plans for children were mentioned, but the implication was that if *Darci* wanted it, she could have it, and not have to sacrifice to get it. Perhaps the supporters of *Dusty* could say that *Darci* was also damaging to personalities by making "superwoman" a goal, but most would say that it is by striving for perfection and falling short that we become the best we can be.

Darci was, in my opinion, the perfect fashion doll. If this is true, then why was she discontinued after just three years? I believe by 1980, most households had several ages of children. Toys were handed down, or at least shared, and *Darci* did not fit into *Barbie*-size clothing. This necessitated the expense of an entire new wardrobe for *Darci*. After years of furnishing children with cases of *Barbie*-size garments, many families simply rebelled against this added play expense. Many, myself included, observed this in

258. Madonna, the music icon of the 1980s, is the inspiration for today's fashion dolls. Like a complete circle, Madonna's Marilyn Monroe image parallels the early teen fashion dolls! *Movie Star News* photograph.

person when shopping for *Darci*. Many children were told that if the doll were brought home, "She would have nothing to wear." Of course, what Kenner had hoped for was just that, except the response would be to PURCHASE the new wardrobe. One must remember that the economic situation in the early 1980s did not often include such an outlay. We collectors, eager to sacrifice grocery money, new clothing or vacations to have the dolls we want, must remember that we are buying these items to love and cherish and not turn over to a child to destroy. Many saw the investment as not worthy of the cost. Adding to the demise of *Darci* was that television advertising was strong at first, but seemed weak later on. By 1980, television was the best source of advertising for a doll; the decision of

Dusty®*Darci*®, *Erica*® and *Dana*® are registered trademarks of Kenner.

259. Hasbro's *Jem* and boyfriend, *Rio*. The story of *Jem* is a complicated one. Highly developed and well thought out, *Jem's* fashions and music tell a wonderful story.

Jem® and Rio® are registered trademarks of Hasbro, Inc.

what toys a child played with were mostly decided by the child and NOT the parent as had been the case in the 1950s.

Clearly the 1980s brought changes to teen fashion dolls. Celebrity dolls (dolls which were made to look like the person intended), became a focal point of collecting. Effanbee's W. C. *Fields* was the first doll in years that was actually sculpted after the character intended instead of created by wigs and clothing. LJN figured if celebrity dolls were selling so well, a celebrity FASHION doll would surely be a hit. Using model Brooke Shields, they issued at Toy Fair, 1982, a *Barbie*-size doll with her likeness. The doll was beautifully made, facially, but the quality of the body, in my opinion, and the neck structure, were not quite right. The slogan of the manufacturer at Toy Fair that year was, "Go For Brooke," urging retailers to "go for broke" and order heavily. The doll,

according to the company, was highly successful, but must have been over-produced, as discount stores carried the doll half price from 1985 on. It still can be found for under $5.00 with some prudent scouting. Again, if the doll interests you, grab it now, as it will be an outstanding collectible of the future. Always a mirror of current trends, fashion dolls became for many children the way to play in the world of outrageous "punk" fashions that they themselves could not risk ridicule by wearing in their own neighborhoods. Many an adult collector of 1980s fashion dolls would come up with the same motive, I am sure. Rock stars like Madonna, Sheena Easton and others manner of "stage" dressing could only be worn every day in some place like New York City. Those children from other towns had to act out this type of dress through doll play.

W. C. *Fields*® is a registered trademark of W. C. Fields Productions, Inc.

Mattel again had a winner with *Barbie and The Rockers*. With so many rock stars denouncing drugs and alcohol, parents seemed more confident to let their children be creative and care-free within limits. *Barbie* as a rock star showed that you could dress outrageously and still be "wholesome." It was like a whole new market had opened up for dolls. Suddenly, just like in the early 1960s, there was room for other dolls. Children, both girls and boys, (the stigma of dolls was easing somewhat for boys) enjoyed playing "rock star band" with this type of doll in shared play.

One company, Creata, issued their own rock star band, *Lace*, in 1986. Their feeling was that just like Whitney Houston is ONE popular singer, there are lots more just as popular. While *Barbie and The Rockers* was one top band, *Lace* could be another! *Lace* featured unnamed girls with outrageous clothing. A black doll, which was especially lovely, featured a 1960s hairstyle in the tradition of the girl groups of the time like the Chiffons. *Lace* is another doll that if the collector is interested in, would do well to purchase right away. One never knows when a rock star, or a rock star doll is going to fade from public view!

The final chapter to our fashion doll anthology was a really serious contender. Hasbro, long known for doing things "right" came up with *Jem*, one of the most fantastic dolls of the 1980s.

Jem had her own story, her own band, her own orphanage, AND her own competition, *The Misfits* built right into her world. With boyfriend *Rio*, and a popular animated series, *JEM* was the first serious competition *Barbie* had had since *Darci* in the late 1970s.

Unfortunately, JEM was withdrawn from the market after a two year trial run. In fact, catalogs and the entire *Jem* line had been designed for 1988. A decision was made to withdraw the doll and go with a "safer" fashion doll, *Barbie* sized, named *Maxie*. The reason *Jem* failed is that like those before her, her larger size meant that clothing already at home for other dolls could not be used on her. Also, her personality of a rock star, singer was one dimensional, and Hasbro executives felt that it had a limited audience. This is all most unfortunate for the collector, for JEM was tailor made for the fashion doll collector. Hasbro's new doll, *Maxie* is basically the concept that *Barbie* was originally founded on...the story of a beautiful teen-age girl and her life. Hasbro has yet to hook a personality on *Maxie*, but if she survives, she will gradually develop into some sort of role as is being planned with a television series, "Maxie's World" which will establish character for the doll.

This new excitement and spirit of competition is catching! The doll collector is the winner, for both companies and other manufacturers as well, will have to pour all their resources into their products lest the competition gain the upper hand. All this only adds to the excitement of fashion doll collecting!

The reader of this anthology has gotten really only a taste of what fashion doll collecting is all about. An exciting new adventure awaits the collector of this type of doll every time he/she enters a toy store! By shopping at doll shows for dolls of the past, and keeping one's collection current, a fabulous panorama of 30 years of history, fashion, pop culture and music can be viewed in three-dimensional form.

Don't YOU want to be a part of this exciting world?

Epilogue

Almost daily, collectors of fashion dolls are reporting new and unusual discoveries in old warehouses, or fascinating current items gathered in travels to other countries.

Because the leader of the pack of fashion dolls is *Barbie*, and because she is the ONLY teen fashion doll to survive a tumultuous three decades, the heart of this book must go to the illustration of the hundreds of dolls and fashions produced by Mattel over the years.

As a teen fashion doll fan, my goal has been to acquaint the collector of this genre of doll with ALL the choices available. The collector of *Tammy* is missing a lot by not knowing *Barbie*. The person who limits their knowledge to just one area loses by not at least viewing the other selection of dolls available. Obviously, space and money are always a consideration in any collection, but this book has attempted to acquaint the novice, and tease the advanced collector with a panorama of teen fashion dolls.

Barbie and other fashion dolls satisfy in a human being the need for continuity in one's life...a feeling that the glorious past and the brillant future are united. Since fashion doll collectors in general, and *Barbie* doll collectors in particular, seem to be upwardly mobile individuals with a strong sense of self worth, it seems safe to say that the teen fashion doll collectors' world is indeed a golden one.

It is difficult to say entirely what has made *Barbie* and these other dolls the inspiration to so many. Psychologists have written many a thesis on the personality of *Barbie*, in particular, and the contribution she has made to our culture.

We, as collectors, can only be thankful that *Barbie*, *Tammy*, *Tressy* and a host of others were there to share our realities and enhance our memories. We hope there will always be *Barbie* and other fashion dolls for a child and a collector to love together.

The Barbie® Family & Friends Tree*

*All of the names present in this chart and the following price guide are protected names. The legal protections were left off for the readability of this chart and the price guide charts.

Relatives

Skipper — Friends
- Ricky
- Skooter
- Fluff
- Tiff
- Ginger
- Scott
- Courtney

Francie — Friends
- Casey

Tutti & Todd — Friends
- Chris
- Dude
- Stacie

Jazzie — Friends
- Chelsea

BARBIE®

Ken — Friends
- Allan
- Brad
- Curtis
- Todd (Groom)
- Derek
- Steven

Friends

- Midge
- Christie
- Stacey
- P.J.
- Jamie
- Steffie
- Kelley
- Cara
- Tracy (Bride)
- Miko
- Dana
- Dee Dee
- Diva
- Whitney
- Teresa
- Bopsy
- Becky
- Belinda
- Kayla
- Deyon

Pets

- Honey
- Midnight
- Dallas
- Pups of Beauty
- Dixie
- Prince
- Tahiti
- Fluff
- Prancer
- Dog 'N Duds
- Dancer
- Beauty

Celebrity Licensed Friends

- Twiggy
- Truly Scrumptious
- Julia
- Miss America
- Donny Osmond
- Marie Osmond
- Jimmy Osmond
- Kitty O'Neil
- Kate Jackson
- Cheryl Ladd
- Debbie Boone
- Kristy McNichol
- Buffy & Mrs. Beasley

Foreign Friends

- Carla
- Valerie
- Chantel Goya
- Flora
- Ellie
- Living Eli (Japan)
- Tulie Chan (Japan)
- Noel (Japan)
- Stephanie (Japan)
- Sophie (Japan)
- Wayne Gretsky
- Bob (Rio version of Ken)
- Kotbie } Korea
- Danbie }
- Lia }
- Diva } Brazil
- Vicky }
- Bobby }

Pet Animals w/O.F.'s or Sets

- Put Ons and Pets — black Poodle
- Put Ons and Pets — Afghan
- Put Ons and Pets — white cat
- Scottie — Skipper's Dog Show
- Dog — Tutti's "Me and My Dog"
- Jamie's grey Poodle
- Jamie's white Poodle

Babies

- Barbie Baby-Sits Baby
- Sears Baby-Sits Baby

Acquaintances

- Lori 'N Rori
- Angie 'N Tangie
- Nan 'N Fran
- Heart Family
  (Mom, Dad, Girl,
  Boy, Baby and cousins)
- Heart Family's
  Grandparents
- Trueheart
  (Heart Family Dog)

International Barbies

- Royal Barbie
- Parisian Barbie
- Italian Barbie
- Oriental Barbie
- Scottish Barbie
- India Barbie
- Eskimo Barbie
- Spanish Barbie
- Swedish Barbie
- Irish Barbie
- Swiss Barbie
- Japanese Barbie
- Peruvian Barbie
- Greek Barbie
- German Barbie
- Icelandic Barbie
- Canadian Barbie
- Korean Barbie
- Mexican Barbie
- Russian Barbie
- Nigeria
- Brazil

Outer Space Friends

- Sun Spell
- Moon Mystic

Teen Fashion Doll Price Guide

by A. Glenn Mandeville

INSTRUCTIONS:
PLEASE READ CAREFULLY!
The prices given are for "Never Removed From Box Dolls," or "Mint in Box Dolls" where applicable. Allow slightly more for a pristine box with no markings, outfits that still have the seal with the outfit name, and ultra mint dolls and packaging. SUBTRACT ONE-HALF of this price for any doll or outfit, no matter how mint, that is missing the box. SUBTRACT ANOTHER 25% if the item is dirty or played with.
BARBIE...
Points to remember when pricing your *Barbie* items.
- Mattel dolls and clothing were mass manufactured by the millions. Only those that are perfectly preserved command top price.
- It is the little accessories to an outfit that make the ensemble complete. The main dress is usually the cheapest part! In *Enchanted Evening* (1960-63) the long, pink satin dress is worth only about $20. The stole is worth $10, the gloves, $5 and the jewelry (a three strand pearl necklace and drop earrings) is worth $15. If this is played with, subtract one-half. The outfit mint in package is worth $100 and up!
- Remember, a guide is just that. Prices given are subject to availability, and do fluctuate from coast to coast. Also, some items are more "popular" than others, and even though list for less, are easier to sell than higher priced items.

- Finally, the way *Barbie* prices are rising, even if you overpay today, it may seem like a bargain tomorrow!

1990 *Barbie*® Price Guide

NAME OF DOLL	NRFB* VALUE
ALLAN	
Bendable Legs	$ 250
Dressed Boxed Doll	$ 350
Straight Legs	$ 65
ANGIE 'N TANGIE	$ 125
BABS	$ 55
BARBIE	
Angel Face	$ 20
Astronaut	$ 15
Baggies	$ 25
Ballerina	$ 25
Beautiful Bride	$ 55
(real lashes)	$ 75
Beauty Secrets	$ 20
1965 Bendable Legs	$ 450
1966 Bendable Legs	$ 800
Bendable Legs (side-part hair)	$2000 up
Black	$ 20
Bubble Cut	$ 175
Busy	$ 95
Busy Talking	$ 95
Color Magic	$ 600
Crystal	$ 20
Day-to-Night	$ 20
Dream Date	$ 15
Dream Glow	$ 15

Dreamtime	$ 15
Dressed Boxed Doll	$ 300 up
Eskimo	$ 65
Fashion Jeans	$ 25
Fashion Photo	$ 25
Fashion Queen	$ 300
Feelin' Groovy	$ 95
Free Moving	$ 95
Funtime	$ 15
Gift Giving	$ 15
German	$ 15
Golden Dream	$ 20
Gold Medal	$ 35
Gold Medal Set	$ 50
Gold Medal Skater	$ 45
Gold Medal Skier	$ 45
Great Shape	$ 15
Growing Pretty Hair	
(pink, 1971)	$ 125
(blue, 1972)	$ 150
Hair Fair	$ 50
Hair Happenin's	$ 500
Happy Birthday	
(white)	$ 20
(pink)	$ 15
Hawaiian	$ 20
Hispanic	$ 20
Horse Lovin'	$ 20
India	$ 65
Italian	$ 175
Japanese	$ 20
Jewel Secrets	$ 15
Kissing	$ 25
Kissing (with bangs)	$ 35
Live Action	$ 75
Live Action On Stage	$ 95
Living	$ 75
Loving You	$ 20
Magic Curl	$ 20
Magic Moves	$ 15
Malibu (1971)	$ 25
My First	$ 15
Newport	$ 35
Number #1 Ponytail	$2500 up
Number #2 Ponytail	$2000 up
Number #3 Ponytail	$ 800
Number #4 Ponytail	$ 400

Oriental	$ 65
Parisian	$ 150
Peaches 'n Cream	$ 15
Pink & Pretty	$ 20
Plus Three	$ 35
Ponytail (1961-1965)	$ 350
Pretty Changes	$ 25
Quick Curl	$ 25
Quick Curl Deluxe	$ 35
Rocker (1986)	$ 15
Rocker (1987)	$ 15
Roller Skating	$ 25
Royal	$ 175
Scottish	$ 125
Sears Celebration	$ 50
Sleep-eyed	$ 525
Standard	
(1967-1970)	$ 225
(1970-1972)	$ 250
Spanish	$ 35
Sun Gold Malibu	$ 15
Sun Lovin'	$ 15
Sunsational	$ 15
Sun Valley	$ 35
Super Hair	$ 15
Supersize	
Beautiful Bride	$ 150
Super Hair	$ 125
Super Star	$ 125
Super Star Fashion	
Change-Abouts	$ 55
In The Spotlight	$ 55
Promotional	$ 75
Swedish	$ 20
Sweet 16	
Promotional	$ 65
Regular	$ 50
Swirl Ponytail	$ 300
Talking	$ 150
Talking Spanish	$ 175
Tropical	$ 10
Twirly Curls	$ 10
Twist 'N Turn	$ 200
Walk Lively	$ 125
Ward's Anniversary	$ 400
Western	$ 20
Wig Wardrobe	$ 150

BARBIE BABY-SITS

SETS	
1963-1965	$ 125
1974-1976	$ 50
BOONE, DEBBY	$ 25
BRAD	
Bendable Legs	$ 75
Talking	$ 75
BUFFY &	
MRS. BEASLEY	$ 125
CARA	
Ballerina	$ 25
Free Moving	$ 25
Quick Curl	$ 25
Quick Curl Deluxe	$ 35
CASEY	
Baggie	$ 35
Twist 'N Turn	$ 75
CHRIS	
1967-1968	$ 95
1974-1976 (Re-issue)	
(European)	$ 75
CHRISTIE	
Beauty Secrets	$ 20
Fashion Photo	$ 35
Golden Dream	$ 25
Kissing	$ 35
Live Action	$ 95
Malibu (1973)	$ 35
Pink & Pretty	$ 25
Sun Lovin'	$ 20
Sunsational	$ 20
Supersize	$ 55
Super Star	$ 35
Talking	$ 125
Twist 'N Turn	$ 125
CURTIS	
Free Moving	$ 35
DANA	
Rocker (1986)	$ 15
Rocker (1987)	$ 15
DEE-DEE	
Rocker (1986)	$ 15
Rocker (1987)	$ 15
DEREK	
Rocker (1986)	$ 15
Rocker (1987)	$ 15

DIVA	
Rocker (1986)	$ 15
Rocker (1987)	$ 15
FLUFF	$ 75
FRANCIE	
Baggie	$ 35
Bendable Legs	$ 150
Black	$ 500
Busy	$ 200
Growin' Pretty Hair	$ 150
Hair Happenin's	$ 175
Malibu (1971)	$ 35
Quick Curl	$ 35
Straight Legs	$ 150
Twist 'N Turn	$ 250
(no bangs)	$ 500
GINGER	
Growing Up	$ 50
JACKSON, KATE	$ 25
JAMIE	
Walking	$ 150
JULIA	
Talking	$ 75
Twist 'N Turn	
(2-piece suit)	$ 95
(1-piece suit)	$ 75
KELLEY	
Quick Curl	$ 55
Yellowstone	$ 150
KEN	
All Star	$ 25
Baggies	$ 35
Bendable Legs	
(old face)	$ 350
(new face)	$ 95
Busy	$ 95
Busy Talking	$ 95
Crystal	$ 20
Day-to-Night	$ 20
Dream Date	$ 20
Dream Glow	$ 15
Dressed Boxed Doll	$ 300
Fashion Jeans	$ 25
Flocked Hair	$ 125
Free Moving	$ 35
Gold Medal Skier	$ 35
Great Shape	$ 15
Hawaiian	$ 25

Horse Lovin'	$	20
Jewel Secrets	$	15
Live Action	$	75
Live Action On Stage	$	95
Malibu (1971)	$	35
Mod Hair	$	55
Now Look	$	35
Painted Hair/		
Straight Legs	$	95
Rocker	$	15
Roller Skating	$	25
Sport 'N Shave	$	25
Sun Lovin'	$	15
Sun Gold Malibu	$	15
Sunsational	$	15
Sun Valley	$	35
Super Star	$	35
Talking	$	65
Talking Spanish	$	75
Tropical	$	10
Walk Lively	$	65
Ward's Dressed	$	95
Western	$	20
LADD, CHERYL	$	25
LORI 'N RORI	$	125
McNICHOL, KRISTY	$	25
MIDGE		
Bendable Legs	$	350
Dressed Box Doll	$	500
Straight Legs	$	125
Wig Wardrobe	$	175
MIKO		
Tropical	$	10
MISS AMERICA		
Quick Curl Blonde	$	25
Quick Curl Brunette	$	45
Walk Lively	$	75
MOON MYSTIC	$	75
NAN 'N FRAN	$	125
O'NEILL, KITTY	$	25
OSMONDS		
Donny	$	25
Marie	$	25
Donny & Marie		
together	$	50

Jimmy	$	35
P.J.		
Baggies	$	35
Fashion Photo	$	35
Free Moving	$	35
Gold Medal Gymnast	$	35
Live Action	$	75
Live Action On Stage	$	95
Malibu (1972)	$	25
Quick Curl	$	25
Quick Curl Deluxe	$	35
Sun Gold Malibu	$	15
Sun Lovin'	$	15
Sunsational	$	15
Sweet Roses	$	20
Talking	$	95
Twist 'N Turn	$	125
RICKY	$	65
SCOTT		
Superteen	$	35
SKIPPER		
Baggie Pose 'N Play	$	35
Bendable Legs	$	225
Dressed Boxed Doll	$	300
Great Shape	$	15
Growing Up	$	35
Horse Lovin'	$	20
Jewel Secrets	$	15
Living	$	35
Malibu (1971)	$	20
Quick Curl	$	25
Quick Curl Deluxe	$	35
Straight Legs	$	50
Sun Gold Malibu	$	15
Superteen	$	25
Re-issue (1970)	$	125
Tropical	$	10
Twist 'N Turn	$	75
Western	$	20
SKOOTER		
Bendable Legs	$	200
Straight Legs	$	95
STACEY		
Talking	$	150

Twist 'N Turn
  (side ponytail) . . . . $ 150
  (short turned up hair) $ 175
STEFFIE
  Busy . . . . $ 95
  Busy Talking . . . . $ 150
  Walk Lively . . . . $ 95
SUN SPELL . . . . $ 75
TIFF
  Pose 'N Play . . . . $ 150
TODD
  1967-1970 . . . . $ 95
  1974 re-issue
  (European) . . . . $ 75
  Sunday Treat Set
  with Tutti . . . . $ 450
TODD (Groom) . . . . . . $ 25
TRACY (Bride) . . . . $ 25
TRULY
SCRUMPTIOUS
  Straight Legs . . . . $ 350
  Talking . . . . $ 350
TUTTI
  Cookin' Goodies . . . . . . $ 400
  Me and My Dog . . . . . . $ 350
  Melody In Pink . . . . $ 300
  Night Night Sleep
  Tight . . . . $ 250
  1967-1971 . . . . $ 95
  1974 re-issue
  (European) . . . . $ 55
  Re-issue Playsettings
  (European) . . . . $ 75
  Sundae Treat Set
  with Todd . . . . $ 450
  Swing-A-Ling . . . . $ 400
  Walkin' My Dolly . . . . . $ 250
TWIGGY . . . . $ 225
WHITNEY
  Jewel Secrets . . . . $ 15
FOREIGN DOLLS OF INTEREST
BARBIE
  Equestrienne . . . . $ 55

Fabulous Fur . . . . $ 35
Golden Nights
  (Disco) . . . . $ 35
Jeans . . . . $ 35
Music Lovin' . . . . $ 35
Playtime . . . . $ 55
Picture Pretty . . . . $ 55
Rio . . . . $ 75 up
Safari . . . . $ 35
Sea Lovin' . . . . $ 35
Snow Princess . . . . $ 250
w/Skooter Gift Set . . . . $ 150
Sporting . . . . $ 95
P.B. (Ma-Ba) . . . . $ 125
BOB
  (Rio version of Ken) . . . $ 150 up
CARLA . . . . $ 55
CHAN, TULIE . . . . $ 350 up
ELLIE . . . . $ 55
FLORA . . . . $ 55
GOYA, CHANTAL . . . . $ 95
GRETSKY, WAYNE . . . . $ 55
KEN
  Golden Nights (35) . . . $ 35
  Jeans . . . . $ 35
  Music Lovin' . . . . $ 35
  Safari . . . . $ 35
  Sea Lovin' . . . . $ 35
SKIPPER
  Golden Nights
  (Disco) . . . . $ 35
  Jeans . . . . $ 35
  Music Lovin' . . . . $ 35
  Safari . . . . $ 35
  Sea Lovin' . . . . $ 35
TAKARA (most notable)
  Excelina . . . . $ 55
  Kansai . . . . $ 150
  Mink . . . . $ 700
  Nakano . . . . $ 200
  Romantic . . . . $ 150
VALERIE
  Hollywood . . . . $ 250
  Tahitiana . . . . $ 250

POPULAR MISCELLANEOUS ITEMS	MINT CONDITION
Airplane	$ 500
Bed, Barbie's Suzy Goose	$ 55
Bed, Skipper's Suzy Goose	$ 55
Car, Barbie's first	$ 55
Cases	$ 20 up
College	$ 225
Deluxe House, Barbie & Skipper's	$ 150
Dream House, Barbie's first	$ 75
Dream Kitchen and Dinette, Barbie's	$ 250
Fashion Shop	$ 125
Furniture, Go-Together (each set)	$ 55
Hot Rod Car, Ken's	$ 75
Little Theatre	$ 225
Piano, Barbie's Suzy Goose	$ 125
Posing Stand, first	$ 300 up
Skipper Dream Room	$ 200
Vanity & Bench, Barbie's Suzy Goose	$ 55
Vanity & Bench, Skipper's Suzy Goose	$ 55

POPULAR GIFT SETS	NRFB VALUE
Party Set	$1200
Mix 'N Match (Ponytail)	$1000
(Bubble-Cut)	$ 750
Trousseau Set	$1800
Fashion Queen Barbie & Her Friends	$ 800
Fashion Queen Barbie & Ken Trousseau	$1200
Barbie & Ken (tennis o/f)	$ 950
Barbie & Ken Little Theatre	$1500
Barbie, Ken & Midge on Parade	$ 950
Barbie, Ken & Midge Pep Rally	$ 500
Barbie's Sparkling Pink	$ 750
Barbie's Round the Clock	$ 750
Barbie's Wedding Party	$1500
Barbie Hostess	$ 800
Midge's Ensemble	$ 500
Skipper Party Time	$ 350
Skipper On Wheels	$ 350

POPULAR SEARS GIFT SETS	
Barbie "Beautiful Bride"	$ 350
Barbie "Movie Groovy"	$ 350
Barbie "Perfectly Plaid"	$ 350
Barbie Travel In Style Set	$ 500
Casey Goes Casual	$ 500
Color Magic Barbie	$1000 u
Francie and her Swingin' Separates	$ 500
Francie "Rise 'N Shine"	$ 500
Malibu Ken "Surf's Up"	$ 350
Live Action P.J. "Fashion 'N Motion"	$ 350
Living Fluff "Sunshine Special"	$ 350
Stacey "Nite Lightning"	$ 850
Stacey "Stripes Are Happening"	$ 800
Talking Julia	$ 500 up
Walking Jamie "Furry Friends"	$ 500
Walking Jamie "Strollin In Style"	$ 500

STORE DISPLAY SETS	$1000 up

CLOTHING (listed by period)	NRFB Value
BARBIE: Early Period 1959-1963	
After 5	$ 100
Apple Print Sheath	$ 75

American Airlines
  Stewardess .... $ 125
Ballerina .... $ 125
Barbie Accessories ...... $ 100
Barbie Baby-Sits
  (apron) .... $ 95
  (layette) .... $ 125
Barbie-Q Outfit .... $ 75
Bride's Dream .... $ 150
Busy Gal .... $ 200
Busy Morning .... $ 75
Candy Striper
  Volunteer (1964) ..... $ 200
Career Girl .... $ 125
Cheerleader (1964) ...... $ 100
Commuter Set .... $ 400
Cotton Casual .... $ 75
Cruise Stripe Dress ...... $ 75
Dinner at Eight .... $ 75
Drum Majorette .... $ 100
Easter Parade .... $2000 up
Enchanted Evening ...... $ 200
Evening Splendour ...... $ 115
Fancy Free .... $ 65
Fashion
  Undergarments .... $ 50
Floral Petticoat .... $ 50
Friday Nite Date .... $ 125
Garden Party .... $ 75
Gay Parisienne .... $1000 up
Golden Elegance .... $ 95
Golden Girl .... $ 55
Graduation .... $ 25
Icebreaker .... $ 100
It's Cold Outside
  (1964) .... $ 75
Knitting Pretty
  (blue) .... $ 100
  (pink) .... $ 100
Let's Dance .... $ 75
Masquerade .... $ 75
Mood For Music .... $ 100
Movie Date .... $ 50
Nighty-Negligee .... $ 125
Open Road .... $ 100
Orange Blossom .... $ 100
Party Date .... $ 125
Peachy Fleecy Coat ...... $ 95

Picnic Set .... $ 125
Plantation Belle .... $ 200
Red Flair .... $ 75
Registered Nurse .... $ 125
Resort Set .... $ 100
Roman Holiday
  Separates .... $ 2000 up
Senior Prom .... $ 125
Sheath Sensation ...... $ 65
Silken Flame .... $ 55
Singing in the
  Shower .... $ 75
Ski Queen .... $ 100
Solo in the Spotlight .... $ 200
Sophisticated Lady ...... $ 200
Sorority Meeting .... $ 125
Stormy Weather .... $ 75
Suburban Shopper ...... $ 125
Sweater Girl .... $ 100
Sweet Dreams .... $ 125
Swingin' Easy .... $ 100
Tennis Anyone .... $ 100
Theatre Date .... $ 125
Wedding Day Set ...... $ 200
Winter Holiday .... $ 100

BARBIE LITTLE THEATRE COSTUMES 1964

Barbie Arabian
  Nights .... $ 175
Cinderella .... $ 200
Guinevere .... $ 175
Red Riding Hood and
  the Wolf .... $ 200

BARBIE TRAVEL OUTFITS 1964

Barbie in Hawaii ...... $ 150
Barbie in Holland ..... $ 150
Barbie in Japan .... $ 200
Barbie in Mexico ..... $ 150
Barbie in Switzerland .. $ 150

BARBIE:

Couture Period 1964-1966

Aboard Ship .... $ 150
Barbie Learns to
  Cook .... $ 150
Barbie Skin Diver ..... $ 75
Beautiful Bride
  (1967) .... $ 375

Beau Time	$ 225
Benefit Performance	$ 500
Black Magic Ensemble	$ 150
Brunch Time	$ 150
Campus Sweetheart	$ 350
Caribbean Cruise	$ 150
Club Meeting	$ 200
Country Club Dance	$ 250
Country Fair	$ 125
Crisp 'N Cool	$ 115
Dancing Doll	$ 200
Debutante Ball	$ 350
Disco Date	$ 125
Dog 'N Duds	$ 250
Dreamland	$ 200
Evening Enchantment (1967)	$ 400
Evening Gala	$ 275
Fabulous Fashion	$ 275
Fashion Editor	$ 250
Fashion Luncheon	$ 500
Floating Gardens (1967)	$ 500
Formal Occasion (1967)	$ 250
Fraternity Dance	$ 350
Fun at the Fair	$ 250
Fun 'N Games	$ 150
Garden Tea Party	$ 115
Garden Wedding	$ 300
Golden Evening	$ 200
Golden Glory	$ 200
Gold 'N Glamour	$ 275
Here Comes The Bride	$ 600
Holiday Dance	$ 200
International Fair	$ 300
Invitation to Tea	$ 350
Junior Designer	$ 150
Junior Prom	$ 250
Knit Hit	$ 125
Knit Separates	$ 95
London Tour	$ 200
Lunch Date	$ 115
Lunch on the Terrace	$ 125
Lunchtime	$ 125

Magnificence	$ 200
Matinee Fashion	$ 275
Midnight Blue	$ 275
Miss Astronaut	$ 500
Modern Art	$ 200
Music Center Matinee	$ 300
On the Avenue	$ 225
Outdoor Art Show	$ 295
Outdoor Life	$ 200
Pajama Party	$ 115
Pan American Airways Stewardess	$2000 up
Poodle Parade	$ 225
Pretty as a Picture	$ 250
Reception Line	$ 375
Riding in the Park	$ 225
Satin 'N Rose	$ 125
Saturday Matinee	$ 275
Shimmering Magic	$ 500 up
Skater's Waltz	$ 200
Sleeping Pretty	$ 200
Sleepytime Gal	$ 200
Slumber Party	$ 200
Sorority Tea	$ 175
Student Teacher	$ 200
Sunday Visit	$ 175
Underfashions	$ 375
Vacation Time	$ 200
White Magic	$ 150

BARBIE: The Mod Period 1967-1971

These outfits are rapidly rising in value. Because of the overwhelming number of outfits produced during this period, fashions are broken up as follows:

	NRFB
A. Street dresses that are unelaborate with few accessories such as Knit Hit, Midi Magic, Snap-Dash, etc.	$ 50
B. Fancy dress sets with lots of accessories that are Mod looking like Zokko!, All That Jazz, Sparkle Squares and Julia and Twiggy fashions also	$ 95
C. Ball gowns and bridal outfits such as Romantic Ruffles, Silver Serenade, Winter Wedding, Let's Have a Ball, etc.	$ 125

BARBIE: The Passive Seventies Period 1972-1976

The 1970s fashions are of much poorer quality. The ones that are collectible are those which correctly show the fashions of the period. Look for outfits like peasant dresses, granny gowns and bell-bottoms!

	NRFB
A. Fashions on blister cards	$ 20
B. Get-Ups 'N Go fashions	$ 25
C. Boxed, fancy, highly accessorized fashions	$ 30

BARBIE: The Disco Daze Period 1977-1979

Disco outfits tell the story of dressing up. The fancy, glittery gowns with boas are the most desirable.

	NRFB
A. Simple dresses	$ 10
B. Designer Originals	$ 20
C. Super Star Fashions	$ 25

BARBIE: The Energetic Eighties Period

Few of the 1980s fashions are yet high priced. Use this opportunity to keep your collection current! Most are only worth original prices. Special outfits that make a fashion statement are priced at double the original price.

	NRFB
A. Collector Series	$ 25
B. Oscar de la Renta Collector Series	$ 25

TAMMY...

Points to remember when pricing *Tammy* dolls and accessories.

- *Tammy* items do surface often mint in box. The doll was overproduced, and much old store stock still survives, almost 25 years later!

- Out of box outfits are actually harder to find than mint in box outfits! There is not much price difference between a mint in box outfit and one complete out of box. The prices given can be used both ways.

- There is, however, still a 50% difference between an out of box doll and one in the box. Mom is worth $45 in the box and $22 out.

• Look for prices on these dolls to rise sharply within the next five years
fashion doll collectors assimilate the rest of the old store stock into the
collections.

Tammy, basic doll in box
  in blue playsuit, complete
  with stand and
  booklet ....$ 50
Pos 'n Tammy ....$ 50
Other editions ....$ 50
Glamour Misty ....$ 35 up
Pos 'N Misty ....$ 35 up
                         $ 50
Mom, Dad, Ted,
  Pepper ....$ 45
Dodi ....$ 55
Pete (hard to find) ......$ 60 up

Tammy's Ensemble Outfits
  Beau and Arrow ....$ 25
  Checkmate ....$ 20
  Cheerleader Outfit .....$ 25
  Cutie Co-Ed...........$ 20
  Dream Boat ....$ 20
  Figure 8 ....$ 20
  Fun in the Sun........$ 20
  Fur 'N Formal ....$ 35
  Knit Knack ....$ 20
  Model Miss ....$ 35
  Picnic Party...........$ 30
  Pizza Party ....$ 35
  Puddle Jumper ....$ 20
  Purl One ....$ 25
  Ring-a-Ding ....$ 25
  School Daze ....$ 25

Skate Date ....$ 25
Sleepytime ....$ 25
Snow Bunny..........$ 30
Sorority Sweetheart ....$ 30
Travel Along ....$ 25
Underwear Outfit......$ 15
Walking Her Pet ....$ 30

1964-1965 Couture
  Outfits ....$ 35 up
Mom Outfits:
  Evening in Paris....... $ 30
  Hidden Glamor .... $ 35
  Lazy Days .... $ 25
  Lounging Luxury ..... $ 20
  Nighty Nite.......... $ 20
  Shopping Topping .... $ 25
Pepper Outfits:
  After School Fun ..... $ 20
  Bed Time .... $ 15
  Class-Room Caper .... $ 25
  Frosty Frolics......... $ 20
  Nylon Undies .... $ 25
  Party Time .... $ 20
Ted and Dad Outfits:
  Clothes on Card
    (sweaters, slacks,
    jackets, trousers,
    shorts, pajamas,
    etc:) .... $ 15 up

Tressy...

Points to remember when pricing *Tressy* dolls and accessories.

• *Tressy* items are the hardest to find mint in box. One almost never sees the
outfits out of box complete, either. American Character did not overproduce
their outfits.

• Gift sets with a doll and makeup or hair accessory are worth double the price of
the single doll.

• *Tressy* dolls, fashions and accessories are destined to be very valuable in the
future. If an item seems a bit high today, buy it anyway as it will be even higher
tomorrow!

Basic Tressy mint in
box .... $ 50

Tressy with posable
knees .... $ 75

Mary Make-Up .... $ 75

Cricket .... $ 45

Hi-Fashion Cosmetic
Kit.................... $ 35

Tressy's Apartment....... $150

Tressy's Hair
Coloring .... $ 25 set

Fashions....

Tressy

Black Magic .... $ 45

Blue Ribbon Winner ... $ 50

Bon Voyage .... $ 50

Campus Casual .... $ 25

Check Mates .... $ 45

Executive Sweet....... $ 35

Fifth Avenue .... $ 45

Good News .... $ 25

Hootenanny .... $ 50

Kitchen Cutie......... $ 45

Lazy Days .... $ 20

Miss American
Character .... $ 50 **up**

Miss Suburbia .... $ 25

Pink Champagne ...... $ 50

Sailing Party .... $ 35

Sugar' N Spice .... $ 15

Window Shopping .... $ 35

Simple dresses on
cards .... $ 10-15

Cricket Fashions

Hootenanny .... $ 25

School Days .... $ 20

Ship Ahoy .... $ 15

Sugar 'N Spice .... $ 20

Windy Weather... ..... $ 15

Judy Littlechap...

Points to remember when pricing *Littlechap* items.

- Mint in box outfits and complete outfits are worth the same price as one seldom sees complete mint outfits.

- Mint in box dolls are worth double out of box price as played with dolls are more common.

- Accessories are really the hard part to find with *Littlechap* outfits. These dolls were overproduced for the demand at the time, meaning old store stock still exists. Make your purchases soon, as these dolls are becoming harder to find every year.

The Littlechap Family

(Mint in box)

Dr. John Littlechap.... $ 50

Judy Littlechap .... $ 50

Libby Littlechap ...... $ 50

Lisa Littlechap .... $ 50

Dr. John's Outfits:

Dr. John's Medical
Outfit................ $ 45

All Weather Coat ..... $ 25

Business Suit .... $ 35

Golf Outfit .... $ 25

Pajamas .... $ 20

Tuxedo .... $ 45

Judy's Outfits:

Bathing Ensemble .... $ 25

Dance Dress .... $ 30

Football Outfit ...... $ 35

Nightshirt .... $ 20

Pajamas .... $ 20

Party Dress	$ 25	Fur-Trimmed Suede	
Red Chesterfield		Coat	$ 30
Coat	$ 30	Lingerie	$ 20
Sportswear Outfit	$ 20	Peignoir and Nightgown	
Three-Piece Suit	$ 30	Ensemble	$ 25

Libby's Outfits:

Three-Piece Chanel

Levis and Sweatshirt	$ 20	Suit	$ 30
Lingerie	$ 15	White Two-Piece	
Pajamas	$ 15	Dress	$ 30
Plaid Reefer Coat	$ 20		

Playsettings:

Three-Piece Blazer		Dr. John's Office	$ 100
Outfit	$ 20	Littlechap Family	
Ya Ya Dress	$ 20	Room	$ 100

Lisa's Outfits:

Littlechap Master

Basic Black Dress	$ 25	Bedroom	$ 100
Formal Evening			
Ensemble	$ 50		

Et Al...

Points to remember when pricing other teen fashion dolls.

• Your eye for quality is the best guide of all. There are dozens of teen fashion dolls that were poor quality. Yesterday's junk is still tomorrow's junk! Just because something is 30 years old does not make it a fine collectible.

• Do not put off till tomorrow what you can buy today. Generic fashion dolls have a very short shelf life. Like cottage cheese, they will be discarded when expired. Make your purchase NOW and avoid disappointment.

• Most fashion dolls are really a bargain. This might not always be the case as more collectors enter the field and supplies decrease. The LJN *Brooke Shields* doll may be on sale in your area now, but in another year or two, be impossible to find!

Brenda Starr dolls...

Basic doll in box	$ 200
with extra wig	$ 250

Dressed dolls in box...

Beach Outfit	$ 200
Shirt waist dress	$ 200
Flower print dress	$ 150
Bride	$ 250
Formals	$ 250 up
extra boxed outfits	$ 50 each,

more for formals

Yolanda (same doll as **Brenda Starr)**

Turquoise satin

formal	$ 250 up
Bride	$ 250
Tulle formal	$ 300

Dusty by Kenner

Dusty doll, basic in

box	$ 25

Skye doll, basic in

box	$ 25

Action set, doll with
sports accessory......$ 35
Fashions .... $ 10 each

Darci by Kenner
Basic Darci ....$ 35
Department Store Special
Darci with extra
dress................$ 50
Dana.................$ 20
Erica................$ 100 up
(very hard to find)
Darci's Van ....$ 50
Darci's Modeling
Studio ....$ 50
Darci's Disco ....$ 50

Darci Fashions:
All That Glitters ......$ 15
Autumn Days ....$ 15
Bermuda Longs ....$ 15
Blue Angels ....$ 15
Bronco Blue ....$ 15
Copper Overalls ......$ 15
Dream Girl ....$ 15
Fancy Dancer ....$ 15
Fancy Pants ....$ 15
Fire Cracker ....$ 15
Garden Gal ....$ 15
Green Light ....$ 15
In the Pink ....$ 15
Jean Scene............$ 20
Mellow Yellow ....$ 15
Party Perfect..........$ 15
Red, White and You ...$ 15
Sheer Delight ....$ 15
Simply Smashing......$ 15
Singin' In The Rain ....$ 20
Slim Jim Girl ....$ 15

Darci Lifestyle Fashions:
Disco Gold ....$ 25
Fur Fantasy...........$ 30
Garden Party ....$ 25
Hi Roller.............$ 25
Lovely Lavender ......$ 25
Plum Perfect..........$ 25
Running Free ....$ 20
Sensational Senorita ....$ 35
Suit Yourself ....$ 25

Perfect Pose Fashions
Blue Lightning ....$ 30
Pink On Point ....$ 30
Wedding Belle ....$ 30

Erica's Outfits
Blushing
Buck-A-Roo..........$ 50 up
Fancy Fleece ....$ 50 up
Plane Sassy ....$ 50 up
Satin Swirls...........$ 50 up

Brooke Shields
Basic Doll in box.......$ 20
Prom Party Brooke
Shields..............$ 35
Suntan Brooke
Shields..............$ 25
Fashions ....$ 10 each

Lace, by Creata. At press time, the beautiful *Lace* dolls and fashions were still available. Once discontinued, they will rise rapidly in value. The first step is usually double the original store price.

Jem, by Hasbro. The world of *Jem* is chock full of future collectibles. The first *Jem* with a blank expression on her face is already a collector's item. The situation here is not that the doll will be discontinued entirely, but each year a new line is shown. Shop BEFORE the Christmas season to find what you want as stores may not get another shipment of this year's items after Christmas. No prices given as the entire *Jem* line minus the #1 *Jem* is still available.